The
Nuremberg
Party
Rallies:
1923–39

Adolf Hitler, Robert Ley, and Rudolf Hess at the 1936 Party Day

The Nuremberg Party Rallies: 1923–39

HAMILTON T. BURDEN

Foreword by Adolf A. Berle

FREDERICK A. PRAEGER, *Publishers*

New York · Washington · London

FREDERICK A. PRAEGER, PUBLISHERS
111 Fourth Avenue, New York, N.Y. 10003, U.S.A.
77–79 Charlotte Street, London W.1, England

Published in the United States of America in 1967
by Frederick A. Praeger, Inc., Publishers

© 1967 by Frederick A. Praeger, Inc.

Material from *The New York Times* © 1933/38 by The New York Times Company.

Library of Congress Catalog Card Number: 67-20473

Printed in the United States of America

FOREWORD

FULFILLMENT OF A DREAM OF EVIL

By ADOLF A. BERLE

It all began in a dingy office in Munich, amid the turbulent bitterness following Germany's defeat in World War I. A group of about forty angry extremists, many of them ex-soldiers, came together and called themselves the German Workers' Party. They soon recruited a handful of ardent nationalists—among them a demobilized soldier by the name of Adolf Hitler.

Hundreds of similar groups were also being organized at that time. The German Workers' Party excelled, if at all, only in the violent intensity of its appeals. However, it steadily gathered strength. In 1920, it changed its name to the National Socialist German Workers' Party. It began to be militant against (it was always "against") Socialists, Communists, and Jews. The party adopted an insignia, the swastika, and a doctrine—that the German government which signed the Versailles Treaty in 1919 was made up of criminals. By 1923, it had obtained a small but substantial national following.

The first authentic party rally was held in January, 1923. Ten years later, in 1933, the party had won a national election, and its leader, Adolf Hitler, had become German Chancellor. By 1943, Hitler, now absolute master of Germany, had conquered most of continental Europe. His power extended from the Volga to the Atlantic, from Norway to Italy. Two years later, Hitler committed suicide in a Berlin bunker as his regime and his party collapsed, crushed by the Allied armies, after involving the entire world in the greatest war in history.

Chronicles, biographies, histories, and accounts of this fantastic period abound. None of them, so far as I know—certainly none in English—has fully analyzed the organizational methods by which this group of fanatical adventurers attained absolute control over Germany in its first decade, and over all Europe in its second. For this reason, I welcome Hamilton Burden's painstaking account of one phase of its methods. Hitler and his associates relied in substantial part on the sheer emotional effect of great party rallies, at which doctrine, ceremony, and ritual were employed to bind men to a single leader and to a common cause. These so-called Party Days are the subject of Burden's study.

They deserve a good deal of thought. For, as Burden's tale unfolds, it is clear that Hitler and his associates—Streicher, Goebbels, and lesser-known figures—combined as diabolical a collection of negatives as could well be imagined. Anti-Semitism, German racism, grievances of defeat, the economic injustices of the Versailles Treaty, the miseries of the German workers—all were used to create a rising tide of hatred. As always, negative emotions can be heated to explosion point when many men who share them come together. Ritual can be used to evoke stereotyped responses. The linking of individual feelings to symbols, drama, music, demonstrations, and ceremonial acts makes it possible to turn hate flames on and off, at predetermined times and places. Are not the procedures of the Ku Klux Klan a minor illustration of the same process? Burden gives us a case history of one aspect of the hate-mobilization process that left Versailles Europe in ruins. Burden's concluding paragraph is an accurate summation:

The Nuremberg rallies . . . are a frightening example of the awe-some power of modern propaganda techniques. Borrowing from pagan cults, church rituals, and Wagnerian theater, and other ways of reaching the thoughts and dreams of the masses, the absolute state perfected, in Nuremberg, its ability to dominate man's mind.

One would like to think that Nazi methods died with Hitler in his Berlin bunker. Perhaps—let us hope so. Unhappily, small groups of power-hungry extremists are still to be found. Grievances, hatreds, emotions, can still be invented, fostered, or exploited. The methods of the Hitler regime can still be imitated. It is appropriate, therefore, to know what they were and how they operated, and to consider how they can be countered.

In retrospect, the Nazi era, even to men like myself who lived through it, seems an evil dream. So, in cold fact, it actually was. The Nuremberg party rallies did not deal in reality. They dealt, quite literally, in passionate and destructive dreams—but dreams that were shared by millions. The final reality, of course, was destruction, death, defeat, and the vast cemeteries to be found throughout contemporary Europe.

Half a century ago, Professor George Herbert Palmer of Harvard adjured his students to beware of their dreams: "They are dangerous things—apt to be fulfilled." Consciously, systematically, with studied dramatic technique, one of the worst dreams in history was nurtured, fulfilled—and, in simple self-defense, destroyed by a world whose civilization, sanity, safety, and existence it had threatened beyond endurance.

All of which must be remembered as we consider the march past, the consecration of the colors, the sanctification of the swastikas—and even the profanation of that noble hymn the "Niederlandisches Dankgebet," written to celebrate the liberation of Amsterdam from Spanish tyranny. May God and history protect us from the acting out of such dreams again; neither, surely, blessed those gatherings at Nuremberg.

PREFACE

The mammoth party rallies at Nuremberg were among the most significant activities of the National Socialist German Workers' Party. The events in Nuremberg were the very heartbeat of the National Socialist movement: nowhere else was the true nature of party ideology shown so clearly and so spectacularly.

Yet the rallies have received little attention from writers on German fascism and the Third Reich. Alan Bullock briefly notes how the rallies intoxicated Hitler, and points out the contrast between the attraction of these gatherings and the mass atrocities concealed behind their façade.[1] Roger Manvell and Heinrich Fraenkel mention the rallies only in passing, although quoting Goebbels on their importance.[2] William L. Shirer does not go into the rallies deeply either; he merely states that they took place and refers to some of the speeches.[3] A survey of the bibliography of National Socialism in English reveals that there is no detailed monograph on the rallies.

The reason for this neglect is perhaps not only the lack of interest of scholars, but also the fact that little source material is available. Since many documents on the criminal acts of the National Socialists have been preserved, it seems likely that the material on the rallies was not deliberately destroyed by the party but was rather lost in the Allied air raids. There are no government papers or documents on the rallies. The only published sources are NSDAP publications and newspapers of the period. The author has made use of much unpublished material secured through private research. Beginning in 1933, *The New York Times* provided extensive coverage of the rallies, and many of the descriptions of Party Day activities that appear in this work are based on reports by that paper's correspondent. The author gratefully acknowledges permission to reprint extracts from this copyrighted material.

In this first attempt at a thorough study in English of the rallies at Nuremberg, I have had the help of many people and institutions. Credit is owed to the staff of the Library of Congress, whose facilities were invaluable, the New York Public Library, and the Archives of the city of Nuremberg. I am grateful to Hans Stegerer and Heinz Boehmler of the Bavarian Radio, who made much unpublished information available to me; to Erwin Kick of Nuremberg; to Stephan Petschek, for establishing valuable contacts for my research; and to Elisabeth Dettmann, for obtaining interesting eyewitness accounts.

My special thanks and appreciation go to Dr. Reinhard Paul Becker, Professor of German at New York University, who has helped me enormously with the intricacies of the German language and with the long and painstaking research that was necessary for this book. I am also grateful to Robert Hale and Julietta Metcalf for their help in organizing and preparing the material. Great thanks are due to Ann Rose Oetiker, without whose continual assistance this book would not have been possible. To my parents I shall always be grateful for their support and their personal suggestions on this project. Finally, to all who gave their advice, I give my personal thanks.

HAMILTON T. BURDEN

New York City
June, 1967

CONTENTS

LIST OF ILLUSTRATIONS*

Endpaper: SA rally at the 1936 Party Day

Frontispiece: Adolf Hitler, Robert Ley, and Rudolf Hess, at the
    1936 Party Day

Page 2: Map of Nuremberg, Party Day of Freedom, 1935

Following page 112:

Party Day medals

Organization Committee

Interior of the Congress Hall

Consecration of the flags at the first Party Day

SA at the 1923 rally

Hitler with Storm Troopers at the 1926 Weimar rally

* PICTURE SOURCES: *Illustrierter Beobachter*; *Reichstagung in Nürnberg* (6 vols.;
Berlin, 1933–38); Leni Riefenstahl, *Hinter den Kulissen des Reichsparteitagfilms*
(Munich, 1935).

The
Nuremberg
Party
Rallies:
1923–39

Nuremberg
Party Day of Freedom, 1935

THE TOWN OF NUREMBERG

N.S.K.K. CAMP
SCHAFFBRÜCKE

CAMP OF THE LABOR SERVICE,
THE S.A., AND THE HITLER YOUTH
LANGWASSER

CAMP OF THE SS
HASENBUCK

CAMP OF THE
WEHRMACHT
GROSS-REUTH

FOLK FESTIVAL

ERLÄUTERUNGEN:
ROUTE OF THE LABOR SERVICE xxxxxxxxx
ROUTE OF THE SA, SS, AND N.S.K.K. ▬▬▬▬

ROUTE OF THE POLITICAL
LEADERS ▬▬▬▬▬▬

RETURN ROUTE OF THE SA AND SS
RETURN ROUTE OF THE N.S.K.K.

1. LUITPOLD ARENA
2. LUITPOLD HALL
3. CONGRESS HALL
4. ZEPPELINWIESE
5. FAIR GROUNDS
6. STADIUM
7. TOWN HALL
8. ADOLF HITLER
   PLATZ
9. KATHARINENBAU
10. APOLLO THEATER
11. KULTURVEREINSHAUS
12. DEUTSCHER HOF
13. OPERA HOUSE
14. RAILROAD STATION

INTRODUCTION: THE CITY OF NUREMBERG

In January, 1923, the National Socialist German Workers' Party held its first party rally in Munich. In September, 1923, it held a second rally, this time in Nuremberg; in 1926, a third rally was convened in Weimar. In 1927, the party once again met in Nuremberg, and all subsequent rallies—the last one was in 1938—were held in that city. The selection of Nuremberg was indicative of the party's determination to make the annual meetings far more meaningful than mere political conventions. Nuremberg was a national symbol; it had been a leading German city from the late Middle Ages to the Renaissance, and in the nineteenth century it emerged as the embodiment of national ideals. The selection of Nuremberg was part of the National Socialists' attempt to create a cult deeply rooted in German national tradition.

In 1050, Emperor Henry III granted Nuremberg permission to establish a mint and a market. In the Middle Ages, a community that acquired these privileges had officially obtained the status of a town and had taken a decisive step toward greater independence from the Reich, both administratively and economically. Nuremberg was under the jurisdiction of the Duke of Swabia until 1127, when Emperor Lothar transferred it to the Duke of Bavaria. Early in the thirteenth century, Nuremberg came under the rule of the counts of Hohenzollern. In 1219, Frederick II conferred upon Nuremberg and other cities the rights of an imperial town. It became a "free town," whose citizens were permitted to ply their trades without interference from the princes. Their only allegiance was to the emperor.

In the free towns, the bourgeoisie had an opportunity to develop freely and acquire independent wealth. These towns were the earliest centers of free enterprise and of the new middle-class culture. Other such towns were Hamburg, Lübeck, and Augsburg, but none became as important as Nuremberg, where an especially creative group of craftsmen, artists, and merchants gathered. Their work earned widespread fame for the town.

In 1360, Nuremberg's outstanding craftsmen discovered a process for wire drawing that was to revolutionize the early stages of German industry. In 1500, the world's first watch was made there by Peter Henlein. The earliest gunstock followed, in 1517, and in 1560 the first brass alloy was processed in the town.

During the Reformation, most big cities violently opposed Luther's new teaching; in 1525, when Nuremberg embraced Protestantism, it became the first imperial town to do so.

In the seventeenth and eighteenth centuries, with the discovery of sea routes to India, world trade flowed away from the city. Although its prominence dwindled, Nuremberg maintained its independence from the petty princes for a surprisingly long time. In 1806, however, Nuremberg was annexed to the state of Bavaria. Until the first third of the twentieth century, the town remained relatively inactive, both politically and economically.

In order to understand the reasons the National Socialists chose Nuremberg, a secondary city, for their annual rallies, one must examine the forces that made it a symbol of national pride. The early economic success of the bourgeois Nuremberger had two immediate consequences for the growth of his city. Like his Dutch counterpart in Amsterdam, the Nuremberg merchant wanted to express his wealth in his style of life—in the appearance of his house and the standards of his household. Since he had not received a classical education (a privilege still monopolized by the nobility and the clergy), he could not base his taste on French or Italian models. So, for example, he built his house in a glorified adaptation of local German style. This was the birth of the famous Nuremberg *Altstadt* (the old part of the town), with its elaborate façades, carved gables, splendidly ornamented Town Hall, and fine wells and doorways.

In the wake of the architectural development of Nuremberg, which had attracted the best stonemasons, carpenters, and other craftsmen from all over Germany, came another development. The citizens of this most beautiful and wealthy city of Germany, by inviting the leading artists and intellectuals of their time to live within their walls, became their most generous patrons.

Of the many artists who lived and worked in Nuremberg at that time, Albrecht Dürer is the most prominent. To the Germans, his greatness lies in having helped to establish an original German tradition in art, one free from the powerful influences of Italy, which then dominated the arts in Europe. Dürer bestowed fame and dignity on German art that would pass far beyond his own time and country. It is through his masterly portraits that we know the visages of some of the leading citizens of sixteenth-century Nuremberg, including Willibald Pirckheimer, the noblest of the Nuremberg humanists. Among the other artists who brought fame to Nuremberg are the sculptors Peter Vischer and Veit Stoss, whose exquisite altars are regarded as the finest works of religious art in German history.

Nuremberg's cultural life reached its peak in the sixteenth century with the *Meistersinger,* local poets who took over the literary forms of the medieval *Minnesang.* Although lacking the genius of their predecessors, they displayed skilled craftsmanship in developing highly intricate verse forms. Soon, though, because of their strong emphasis on form, the movement was stranded in mannerism and pedantry.

During the seventeenth and eighteenth centuries, Nuremberg was largely ignored by German society. The reasons for its loss of prestige are readily seen. The late seventeenth and early eighteenth century were ruled by the ideas of the Enlightenment, which recognized classical examples as the only worth-while ones in the arts and sciences. New generations in Germany were brought up exclusively in the classical tradition; to be educated meant to understand and appreciate classical philosophy and classical architecture, and to be able to read the classical authors.

The German educated class despised their native culture as home-spun, boorish, and crude. The word "Gothic" was applied to it, with the meaning "barbaric." Cities that boasted typical German architecture, such as Nuremberg, were completely forgotten. The petty princes of the eighteenth century built their small German residences after the model of Versailles, or imitated Greek and Roman styles. Those cities that adjusted themselves in their outward appearance to the taste of the time became centers of cultural life. In the seventeenth century, Cologne and Heidelberg were such centers; in the eighteenth century, Dresden, Strasbourg, and Leipzig. Intellectuals in these cities gathered to study antiquity; many of them crowned their endeavors with a pilgrimage to Italy, the land of ideal classical beauty.

It was not until the end of the eighteenth century that Nuremberg was rediscovered. During the 1770's and 1780's, many Germans had grown increasingly discontent with the foreign influences in art and literature, and even in social life. More and more voices demanded liberation of German taste from French and Italian models; young men wanted a place for a genuine German tradition, and they began to satirize their elders, who, they felt, were trapped in a now stale and lifeless classical tradition.

In the spring of 1796, two young students at Berlin University, Ludwig Tieck and Heinrich Wackenroder, set out during their spring vacation for a hiking trip into southern Germany. Neither of them had ever been south of the river Main. They were immediately enchanted by the beauty of the hills and valleys of this vineyard country, but it was not until they entered the gates of Nuremberg that they experienced the greatest revelation of their lives. They had been born and brought up in Berlin, a city designed in a neoclassical style, built by the father of Frederick the Great. In Nuremberg they saw for the first time an entire city built in the old, original German-Gothic style. When they returned home, they collaborated on *Die Herzensergiessungen eines kunstliebenden Klosterbruders* (1797), an enthusiastic testimony to the great beauty to be found in the German past in general, and in Nuremberg in particular. The German public was immediately captivated by the freshness and sincerity of their praise:

O Nuremberg, thou once world famous city! With what childlike eyes did I revel at thy quaint houses and churches which bear the

visible imprint of our old patriotic art! How dearly do I love the
creations of that time which speak such an outright powerful and
true language. How do they lure me back into that great century,
when thou, Nuremberg, were the lively throbbing school of our national art and a fertile overflowing spirit lived and worked within
thy walls. . . . Oh I know them, the laurel groves of Italy, I know
it well, the heavenly glow of the enthused men of the fortunate
South: why do you call me away from here? Do not Rome and Nuremberg lie on the same earth?

This book rekindled the interest of the Germans in their national heritage, and as Tieck and Wackenroder hoped, the redis-
covery of Nuremberg reconciled Germans with their own culture
and freed them from their dependence on foreign influences. Now
the German Romantics could embrace German tradition and
study their own past for inspiration and aesthetic examples.
Throughout the nineteenth century, Nuremberg grew in national
esteem as a sanctuary of German culture. It is interesting that
when the first German railroads were built, Nuremberg was the
first town connected with the system, in 1835.

The newly awakened interest in *das Altdeutsche* ("old German
things") was further stimulated by Ludwig Tieck's novel *William
Lovell* (1798). The book describes the formative years of a young
painter in Nuremberg who was so deeply impressed by the atmosphere of that city that he built his whole career and artistic
development on this great German style. The architecture stimulated not only his work but that of the greatest masters of his
time in Nuremberg—including that of his teacher, Albrecht
Dürer. In this book, Nuremberg took on the role that Rome or
Florence had formerly played in the imagination of artists.

The Romantic view of Nuremberg persisted in Germany
throughout the nineteenth century. Later in the century, when
Richard Wagner was choosing material for his operas from German myths and folk epics, he included the legend of Nuremberg.
Audiences as well as critics considered *Die Meistersinger von
Nürnberg* his most successful opera. When he brought on stage
sixteenth-century Nuremberg, with its skilled craftsmen and ar-
tisans, its carefree apprentice boys, and its dignified and wealthy
burghers, Nuremberg as a symbol of German culture reached its
zenith in the imagination of the German people.

The first Nazi party congress called by Hitler was held in

Munich, in 1923, because the party originated in that city. But
when the National Socialists considered holding large-scale and
spectacular party rallies, they realized that the selection of a
locale was of great importance. In conversations, Hitler mentioned his selection of Nuremberg:

> Had I so wished, I could have arranged for the party congresses to
> take place in Munich. But as I wished as many towns as possible—
> big, medium, and little—to participate and to become centers of Ger-
> man cultural life, I suggested to the party committee that we should
> choose Nuremberg for our rallies, and our annual gathering there
> must, I think, give the city for ten days the atmosphere of the Olym-
> pic Festival of ancient days.[1]

According to Fritz Nadler, a Nuremberg journalist and author,[2]
Julius Streicher claimed to have first suggested Nuremberg as a
congress city. Streicher was at that time a schoolteacher and leader
of the National Socialist party in Nuremberg; later he became
Gauleiter of Franconia.

The National Socialists were well aware of the national and
historical significance this city would lend to their rallies. An editorial published in the *Völkischer Beobachter* a few days before
the first Nuremberg rally commented that "in few cities does the
contrast between past and present find so precise an expression as
in Nuremberg—turrets, mighty walls and towers give testimony of
manly power and fighting spirit."[3] A leading motif of the party's
early efforts shows through clearly here: the attempt to lend dignity to the present by reveling in a glorious past, thereby winning
the masses to a belief in the great National Socialist future. The
fighting spirit that the journalist saw expressed in Nuremberg's
medieval walls and towers was, indeed, of great importance to the
Nazis. The old castle in Nuremberg particularly impressed Hitler.
From the beginning of German history, it had been a bulwark
against foreign intruders, a symbol of courage. For the Nazis, it
became a milestone on the way to German freedom and independence, as revealed in Hitler's remarks:

> It has . . . been reasonably and firmly established that the origin
> of Nuremberg was an old Salic castle, round which, little by little, a
> village grew. Most medieval cities were founded in the same way;
> hence the large number of towns created during the Middle Ages

in Eastern Germany. These fortress castles were of great importance for the protection of the peasantry. Without them, the country folk would never have been able to maintain themselves against the oriental hordes which even overran our territories. In Transsylvania, where these fortresses were not so numerous, fortifications had to be constructed against, among others, the Turks, and this explains why one frequently finds that even the churches are designed to resist attack.[4]

Once it was decided that the party rallies would be held in Nuremberg, the Nazis started a large-scale campaign to publicize the city all over Germany. Photographs of famous Nuremberg buildings appeared by the thousands in every German newspaper and magazine. Every aspect of the city was exploited to present the new Nazi theme, the fusion of past and present as seen in the modern rallies held in historic "Old German" settings. German history itself had provided the Nazis with a magnificent stage; on it, during the course of the next fifteen years, would take place the most breathtaking and demonic displays the world had ever seen.

1   THE FIRST PARTY DAY
                    1923

It is customary for nations and political parties to celebrate the
date of their origins and great moments in their history. The Nazis
were no exception; they commemorated, for instance, November
9 (the date of the Munich *Putsch*) and January 30 (the day of their
accession to power in Germany). It is surprising, then, that the
first official Party Day was never emphasized by National Socialist
historians and propagandists. Although it was meant to be the first
in a long series of party congresses, party members failed to point
it out as the start of an important tradition, and this initial meeting, on January 27 and 28, 1923, never became a milestone in
National Socialist history. Perhaps the Nazis, despite their claims
to the contrary, felt at that time much as Stephen H. Roberts did
when he wrote: "Little was done at this congress, and nothing indicated that it was a precursor of a long series."[1]

The results of the first party congress are not entirely clear, because of the lack of documentation on this early period. It can be surmised that the original purpose of the congress was to bring together all the party members in order to demonstrate the strength of the organization and to win popular support. Nevertheless, upon closer inspection, this rally seems at least as important as the subsequent ones, because of its innovations in the techniques of political propaganda.

Alan Bullock sees as the main force behind the 1923 rally Hitler's fear that Germany might unite behind the present government in the face of the French occupation of the Ruhr: "To make people listen to him, Hitler summoned 5,000 of the SA, or Storm Troopers, to Munich for a demonstration at the end of January, 1923."[2]

But there were also other forces behind the events that led up to the first Party Day. The comparative tranquillity of prewar German political life had been completely shattered in 1918 by the abdication of Kaiser Wilhelm II and the signing of the armistice with the Allies. For years, discontent with the Kaiser's leadership had mounted steadily, from the members of the General Staff and the Reichstag down to the masses. The centuries-long rule of the Hohenzollern emperors suddenly gave way to a multiple-party system that brought the nation close to a state of anarchy. The positions of the political parties ranged from the extreme nationalistic, militaristic right through the Catholic center to the extreme left. The violent activities of these many factions led Germany to the brink of civil war.

After his recovery from injuries received in World War I, Hitler was assigned to a job as an instruction officer in the Press and News Bureau of the political department of the Army's Seventh District Command. In the course of his duties, he was selected to attend a meeting of the German Workers' Party in Munich. This party had been founded by Anton Drexler, who intended it to represent both the working class and the nationalists; when Hitler joined, the party had only forty members, though there were many similar groups in Germany, varying in their degree of nationalism, militarism, and anti-Semitism. After attending the meeting, Hitler decided to join the group. Soon he gained considerable influence in the party's affairs; gradually he came to exercise total power over it.

The most successful of the other rival nationalist groups at that
time was the Austrian Deutsche Nationalsozialistische Arbeiterpartei (German National Socialist Workers' Party), founded in
1910 by Dr. Riehl. The DNSAP set up an inter-state bureau with
offices in Vienna and the Sudetenland. It was this bureau that invited the cooperation of the Bavarian National Socialists. In 1920,
the Munich party adopted the title of the Austrian party, with
only a change in the word order: it became the Nationalsozialistische Deutsche Arbeiterpartei (National Socialist German
Workers' Party), or NSDAP.

One of the leading members of the party at that time was Major Ernst Roehm, who was indispensable in securing the protection of the army and of the Bavarian Government, which
depended on the local army command as the ultimate arbiter of
public order.[3] Roehm also recruited new members for the party
from among former members of the Freikorps (Free Corps) and
other war veterans.

These new members formed the nucleus of the SA. Many of
the party's most important members joined during these early
years; among them were Rudolf Hess, Hermann Goering, and Alfred Rosenberg. Dietrich Eckart, who was to become the first
editor of the *Völkischer Beobachter*, significantly influenced Hitler in these years and helped him to raise money for the party.
Important because of their later association with the rallies were
two other men who also joined at this time: Heinrich Hoffmann,
the official party photographer, the only man who was allowed to
photograph Hitler and the publisher of pictorial booklets on
each of the major party rallies of the 1930's, and Max Amann,
an old war friend of Hitler's—in fact, his former sergeant—who
became Hitler's business and publishing manager.

Within a very short time, the party headquarters grew from a
dingy back room without furniture or telephones into a well-
equipped, efficient center for party activities.

Outside events worked in favor of extremists in these years.
Because of the high reparations payments fixed by the Allies, the
German government found it impossible to get popular support.
There followed such inflation that the government was forced
to ask the Allies for a moratorium on reparation payments. Public
dissatisfaction found its most violent expression in the assassination of several important government figures by extremists.

Since the SA played such a prominent role in the development of the party and its rallies, its origin and early growth should be mentioned here. The SA was informally created in the summer of 1920 to combat the party's many opponents; it was officially founded on August 3, 1921, when a so-called gymnastics and sports division was formed inside the party. After October 5, of the same year, it changed its name to Sturmabteilungen, or Storm Troopers. The usefulness of the SA was demonstrated in October, 1922, when Hitler took 800 of them to Coburg for a nationalistic demonstration and fought a fierce battle in the streets against the Socialists and Communists. The participants regarded their fight as an honorable service to the party and a medal was struck in commemoration of the event.

It was during these years that the swastika, which was to become so important in the stage setting of the rallies, made its first appearance. The symbol can be found in several cultures, ancient and modern, in various parts of the world. In the years 1918–19, German troops came upon it in Finland. The Erhard Brigade wore it painted on their helmets when they marched into Berlin during the Kapp *Putsch* in the spring of 1920. Hitler also may have seen it in his youth as a symbol among the anti-Semitic parties of Austria.

The many designs submitted to Hitler for a symbol of the National Socialist Party and for a flag always included the swastika. Hitler says in *Mein Kampf* that the selection of the colors and the swastika was his own idea. He had rejected black, red, and gold as the hated colors of the Weimar Republic; he preferred the old imperial colors—black, white, and red—since, he said, the red stood for the social idea of the movement, the white represented the nationalist idea, and the swastika was reminiscent of the struggle for the victory of Aryan man.

Despite gains in its first three years of existence, the NSDAP was still a local party in southern Germany, with little or no support outside of Bavaria. Hitler and his followers could not win power alone. He needed support from other groups with similar political inclinations. It was to attract the attention of such groups and of the general public that the first Party Day was held.

Hitler characterized the party rallies of the 1920's as *"erweiterte Generalmitgliederversammlungen"* ("enlarged general assemblies of all members"), or simply as *"Parteitage"* ("Party Days"), in which not all the country but only Bavaria was represented.[4] Actually, however, this is not entirely true of the first Party Day, because other parts of Germany and even foreign countries were represented. The spirit of this first party rally is well expressed in a proclamation Hitler published in the *Völkischer Beobachter* of January 27, 1923. Here he set forth his own views on the defeat of Germany in World War I, the rise of Marxism, the threat of France, and the weakness of the Weimar Republic. He made a strong appeal to the public to join the National Socialists, in order to cope with the problems facing Germany.

Hitler's theory on the reasons for Germany's defeat in World War I—the stab-in-the-back theme—which was to be repeated endlessly in the years to come, was already strongly voiced in the January 27 statement. Not even the shortage of weapons and ammunition was accepted as the cause of defeat. "It is not the piece of metal a soldier has in his hands that is important. The will to fight a good battle and to win the war is the decisive factor. The cause of our defeat was the poisonous theory of Marxism. Soldiers cannot win battles if human dignity is denied and if they are engaged in the social class struggle."[5] After having thus exonerated the German people of their responsibility for the lost war, he went on to absolve the military leadership:

What brought about Germany's total defeat in 1918? Was it the greater strength of the Allied army or the superior leadership of their armed forces? That most certainly was not the case: strength, energy, will power and determination are decisive factors. In military leadership the German Army was superior to its enemy. If strength alone had been the deciding factor, the war would have been ended by 1915 or 1916, especially as our enemies possessed a much larger army. It was only the superior leadership of the German military leaders that enabled us to keep on fighting for four and a half years.[6]

Hitler then continued his analysis of Marxism and its effects on the German people: "The theories of Marxism have already made a deep impression on our people. Authority is disregarded, the creative powers of the personality are hemmed in, leadership is discredited, and the democratic principles of majority laws are destroyed while the weak, evil, cowardly, and irresponsible masses have to be considered all-important. In our society personality is murdered by the mute masses."[7]

Hitler then proceeded to blame Marxism for the economic setbacks of postwar Germany. He also chastised the Germans for lack of national self-respect. "Belief in our national rights and will power are very low, while in their place is the insane hope that love and forgiveness will be the basis of the newly created peace of the world. This hope merely weakens the fighting spirit of the 70 million German people and allows them to be lured by American big business."[8] The callous cynicism with which Hitler used the words "love" and "forgiveness," as if they represented a shameful weakness, is a good example of his technique of deliberately distorting the meaning of words in order to destroy his listeners' sense of moral values.

He continued: "As long as the will to free ourselves from all bonds is not nation-wide, we will not be able to achieve our goal."[9] Then he threatened retaliation against all his political opponents, both inside and outside Germany, and claimed that only the National Socialist Party could lead the Germans to freedom. With this proclamation, published only two days before the beginning of the first party rally, Hitler expressed the tenor of that congress.

The 1923 rally had been planned long in advance. On January 11, 1923, the party demonstrated against the so-called November criminals.* In the following weeks the party called for a rally in Munich. There had been previous meetings of all Bavarian members in the years 1920–22. This Party Day, however, was to represent members from all over Germany and from abroad, and the Bavarian government apparently sensed the importance of the congress. Chief Constable Nortz proclaimed a state of emergency and permitted only six of the planned twelve meetings. Despite this order, the party held all twelve meetings under the pretext that there was not time enough to cancel the six. The government of Bavaria was later heavily criticized for having tolerated the party meetings at all.

The *Völkischer Beobachter* of January 31, 1923, gives an interesting account of the political atmosphere in Munich on the eve

_____

* This was the standard name in party terminology designating the groups and individuals inside Germany who pleaded for Germany's capitulation in 1918. Hence the stab-in-the-back legend of the German nationalists.

of the first Party Day. Red and yellow posters informed the citizens of the town that the Reichstag had declared a state of emergency. Rumors circulated throughout Munich that a *Putsch* was planned. One reaction to this tension in Munich appeared in the *Bayrischer Kurier* of January 28, 1923: "The Social Democrats have alerted their party members and their followers. In the last few days Munich has become the scene of an ugly party battlefield." It was also rumored in Berlin that the National Socialists had threatened to use force when the police commissioner refused them the use of a public square for the Fahnenweihe ceremony (consecration of the flags), one of the earliest rituals of the young party, during which new banners were initiated for new party factions by touching them with the original flag of the party.

The participants in the rally arrived by train from all parts of Germany. In Stuttgart, the railroad authorities refused to furnish a special train for the party members' trip to Munich. In Gera, party members were taken off the train and arrested, and in Nuremberg a special train was stopped and not allowed to continue.

A reception was held for the out-of-town members at the Fürstensalon in Munich. From there the groups marched to their quarters or to the Hofbräuhaus Festsaal (ceremony hall of the Hofbräu House), where the rally headquarters were located. In the evening, meetings were held for members in various parts of the city.

The general themes of these meetings were: What has to be done in Germany? What do the National Socialists want? In the Hofbräuhaus, Dietrich Eckart was the speaker. He compared the NSDAP to the Social Democratic Party. Eckart said that National Socialists would never stand united with the "November criminals." He pointed out that the "newly found nationalism" of the Social Democrats was as fraudulent as the statements of the *Bayrischer Kurier,* which claimed that National Socialism was fighting the Catholic Church. He branded these accusations as lies and slander.

The proceedings of this first Party Day show that even at this early time, annexation of the German-speaking territories in Europe was being considered. Prodinger,* from Salzburg, spoke of the desire and willingness of the German-speaking Austrians to

---

* In many cases, it has been impossible to learn the full names of minor party officials and other individuals connected with the rallies. Thus, throughout the book, certain individuals will be identified by last name only.

help fight the enemies of the party. A National Socialist representative from Prague, Simm, expressed himself in a similar way. He
described the hardships of the German people of Czechoslovakia,
who lived, he said, almost like slaves. He voiced their hopes that
the National Socialists would bring about the greatly desired
Gross-Deutschland, or Great Germany.

After Simm, other members of the party, representing various
parts of the country, took the rostrum and spoke briefly on different aspects of National Socialist goals.

The climax of each meeting was Adolf Hitler's address. When
Hitler spoke at the Münchner Kindl cellar, approximately one
thousand people carrying some ninety flags were gathered there to
hear him.

He referred sarcastically to the recent problems between the
party and the Reichstag, flatly denying any intention of a *Putsch*
on the part of the National Socialists. "The present Reichstag is
actually helping our party. Through its lack of action, new members are recruited for the party every day. Our Reichstag is so
weak that no *Putsch* is needed. In due time it will collapse—a
slight breeze could accomplish this."[10]

He went on to chastise the local authorities for having made arrival in Munich difficult for party members. There was some quib-
bling about intra-party disagreements, and then Hitler said: "After
our reckoning [with foreign and domestic enemies] we will divide
the people into Germans and non-Germans. The German traits
will be successful, and we will destroy what is non-German."[11]

Hitler was never blunter in expressing his real plans than he
was in these first meetings. For diplomatic reasons, once he gained
power, he could not afford to be so frank. In the 1930's he played
the role of the peace-loving father of the nation because it served
his diplomatic purposes; but during the first Party Day, he spoke
freely, as the visionary with no responsibility.

At the end of the meeting, the following resolutions were
passed:

1. The Versailles Treaty was to be declared void at once.

2. War-debt payments in materials or money were to be stopped.

3. The German monetary system had to be reformed immediately.

4. A new law was needed to protect the fatherland against
traitors.

5. The protection law (*Schutzgesetz*) must be suspended, setting

free all national "defenders"; the "November criminals" must be arrested.

6. An effective law had to be passed that provided the death penalty for usurers and profiteers.

According to the *Völkischer Beobachter,* the meeting lasted almost until midnight. The party members were asked to leave quietly and not to form parades, for the enemies of the party would welcome the chance to harass them. There were no disturbances. After the SA had gone to their quarters, the police returned to their posts. Munich was silent.

The following day was devoted to the public spectacle of the consecration of the flags. Again, one must turn to the *Völkischer Beobachter* for an account of the ceremony; there is no question that its accounts are strongly biased, but it is the only source for reconstruction of the events.

Long before the first Storm Troopers arrived for the ceremony, huge crowds of spectators had assembled on the Märzfeld. An estimated 15,000 to 20,000 people eventually gathered for the consecration. To avoid clashes with the police, the participants refrained from marching through the center of town on their way to Märzfeld. Each group followed a flag, and though no weapons were carried, the parade to the field was reminiscent of a military ceremony. At 11:00 A.M., the Storm Troopers were assembled in the field. A few commands were given, and the bands played the chorale "Niederländisches Dankgebet."

The consecration ceremony officially began with an address by Adolf Hitler. He began by explaining the symbolism of the colors on the new flag—black, white, and red; he then expressed the hope that these colors would always be a symbol of Germany's greatness and power. Once again he used the opportunity to lash out at the Jews, by proclaiming that no Jew would ever be allowed to touch the Nazi flag. After this brief address, the bands played a military march, and hundreds of banners were lowered for the consecration. Hitler administered the vow to the SA, who had to swear they would not abandon the banner under any circumstances.

After the ceremony, Major von Xylander addressed the SA men in the name of the brother organization Völkischer Rechtsblock (Nationalist Right) of Bavaria. He pointed out that the two organizations were fighting shoulder to shoulder against their enemies, France and Judaism. Next followed the parade of the Storm

Troopers. As Hitler watched, the men marched by in groups of a hundred. This first parade lasted about forty-five minutes. The ritual consecration of the flags and the march became traditional at all future congresses.

That night, gala meetings were held throughout Munich. The excitement of the consecration ceremony seemed to linger, and the various meeting halls were filled to capacity; in fact, one had to be closed to new arrivals. The meetings were addressed by speakers of little significance. After the speeches in the Hofbräu- haus, Richard Wagner's *Rienzi* Overture was played. This espe- cially pleased the artists and intellectuals who had joined the meeting. It is interesting to note that even on this first Party Day, Wagnerian effects—so elaborately employed in the later rallies— were already being used.

On Monday, January 29, about three hundred leaders of the local party groups from all German-speaking territories met to hear Hitler's address. He first described Germany's political situa- tion in national and international affairs, and then presented the following precepts of the National Socialist movement:

1. A sense of responsibility toward the nation must be based on duty. German civil servants and soldiers are prime examples of groups inspired by this sentiment. Although these men are by no means overpaid, they always unselfishly put the interest of the na- tion above their own.

2. For the German people, the national idea is identical with the social idea. The more strongly nationalism is emphasized, the more concern there must be for the welfare of the people.

3. Anti-Semitism is a refutation of the known enemies of the nation. Nationalism is basically a precaution against the Jewish plague. If unchecked, Judaism would poison the national and so- cial ideas of the people.

Hitler then spoke about the fight for supremacy between the elite and the masses. This fight, he said, extended into politics and the economy. If the masses should win supremacy, they would de- stroy the German race and culture. He again blamed the Versailles Treaty for the nation's problems. He pointed out the injustice Germany was suffering at the hands of the French in the Ruhr Valley and asked the death penalty for the "November criminals." He attacked Communism: "We shall make no concessions to the 'Internationale'—they will have to go along with us or we shall push them out of the way. We shall divide everything into German and anti-German; National Socialists will never forgive their enemies."[12]

As his speech drew to a close, he was carried away by his own fanaticism and made a statement that was to assume macabre truth, although not in the way he intended: "We want history to show that all traitors were convicted in our trial. This trial will be remembered for centuries."[13] He then expressed the extreme readiness of the movement to enforce its ideas.

The effect of statements such as these on his audiences must have been particularly powerful. It was true that Germany was suffering under the burden of the Versailles Treaty. It was true that many Germans who had no connection whatever with the party deeply resented the presence of French troops in the German Ruhr Valley. And it was true that Communism presented a danger to German society. Unfortunately, many nonpartisan Germans who heard Hitler publicly criticize these conditions may have been won over to him solely because they shared his views on these problems.

Also on Monday, a meeting of the party members was held. Hitler was there to open it. He reported on the nation-wide growth of the party and mentioned that the local party of Munich had the largest membership. Anton Drexler, the founder of the party and honorary president of the meeting, began to speak on the history of the movement, but he was so exhausted from the exertions of the rally that he was unable to continue. He asked Hitler to speak in his behalf. Hitler said that it was Drexler's idealism that convinced him to join the party. According to Hitler, the first mass meeting was held on February 25, 1920. The party was opposed, he complained, with every known measure—silence, ridicule, and slander. However, during the year of 1921, he continued, the achievements of the party could be seen in Germany and abroad.

After Hitler's speech, the party's financial secretary, Singer, gave a short report on the National Socialists' financial situation. He stated that the figures on the party books were now in the millions, and thanked all members for their contributions—especially those from financially depressed areas.

Next, a party member by the name of Hermann Esser spoke on the importance of the newspaper *Der Völkischer Beobachter*, the official party organ. He said that the party had realized from the

beginning the necessity of having a resolute party organ, unafraid
to tell "the whole truth." He pointed out that the *Völkischer
Beobachter* had long since become a national newspaper and
added that it was the job of the press to expose the slanderous
statements of the enemy newspapers. Hitler then thanked Dietrich
Eckart for his sacrifices on behalf of the *Beobachter,* and Rosenberg for his assistance in systematically planning the rally program.

Anton Drexler then presided over the election of a new executive committee. Hitler was unanimously voted chairman, and was
asked to designate the members of his committee. He named
Jakob second chairman, Singer and Tripps financial secretaries,
Briemann and Schwaiger secretaries, and Koerner propaganda
chairman. The party members unanimously elected these men to
the committee. It is interesting that most of the men elected to
important positions at the first rally were not significant in the
years the Nazis held power.

The following resolutions were proposed for the coming months:
suspension of all deliveries to France, stabilization of the mark,
nationalization of the banks, liberation of the national "defenders," and tougher prosecution of traitors, usurers, and profiteers.
These resolutions are practically the same as those passed two days
before, at the meeting of January 27.

An Austrian, Gatterer, addressed the meeting in the name of
the German people of Austria. He said the achievements of the
NSDAP would be an inspiration for his people. The next speaker
was Ernst Patzel from Czechoslovakia. He brought greetings from
his people and spoke of the growth of the NSDAP among them.
Seifert, from the city of Hanover, addressed the members from
those provinces outside of Bavaria where the party was banned.
To be prepared to fight, he said, was of primary importance. Hitler then spoke again, vigorously protesting the opposition the
party was experiencing in some parts of Germany.

During these days the *Völkischer Beobachter* had been covering
the rally very closely. In the issue of January 31, the paper summed
up its impressions:

The third day of the party rally of the NSDAP has come to an end.
Although some party members were not allowed to travel, were
forcefully taken off trains, had the iron crosses ripped from their

uniforms, although the government tried to prohibit the ceremonies and declared a state of emergency—still the Party Days were held. Two brigades of German men marched with their banners through the city of Munich. The swastika will be the national symbol of the future Germany. All party members swore to be true to the party and to the man who leads and guides them. The German spirit cannot be broken in these men. Germany is awakening. The German freedom movement is on the march. The name of this movement is the NSDAP. Heil!

The ritual of all future party congresses was set in this first meeting, and most of the extremist ideas of National Socialism—anti-Semitism, the annexation of German-speaking territories, the ruthless destruction of the enemies of National Socialism —were expressed by Hitler on the first Party Day. No one can say that Hitler attempted to hide his intentions from the German people with promises of a better life in the course of a general national recovery. The conflicts with the government and the fanatic political atmosphere, characteristic of all the rallies of the 1920's, were heavy in the air even at this early time.

GERMAN DAY
1923

From the point of view of the National Socialists, the rally of January, 1923, had been a complete success. They had staged it despite serious government opposition; they had managed to avoid major incidents with the authorities; they had dealt with their business as a political party; they had proved to their members and to the general public that they were seriously striving for power.

The bitter discussion of Germany's responsibility for reparation payments, the desperate economic plight of German citizens, and the uneasiness over the presence of French troops in the Ruhr Valley had grown considerably in the months after the rally. It must have seemed to the National Socialists that the tide of events was turning in their favor, and that it was a good time once again to demonstrate publicly. A patriotic pretext for a second party congress was easily found—the anniversary of the victory of the

Prussian Army over the troops of Napoleon III at Sedan in September, 1870. Therefore a second rally was scheduled for September, 1923, and at Hitler's request it was held at Nuremberg—the city that had once been host to the pageantries of the Holy Roman Empire.

According to National Socialist authors, the city council of Nuremberg did everything in its power to prohibit or limit the German Day rally. Julius Streicher and Willy Liebel, later to be mayor of Nuremberg, organized the meeting. In the September 2 issue of the *Völkischer Beobachter,* much was made of an earlier Communist youth rally in Nuremberg, which had run into serious difficulties with the police. The newspaper pointed out that the mayor of the city, Dr. Luppe, had endorsed this meeting by decorating the town in honor of the Communist congress. There had been several unruly demonstrations and incidents of mob violence, and the citizens of Nuremberg, as well as some members of the city government, had been unnerved by the congress.

The *Beobachter* proudly claimed that the citizens paid even more attention to the National Socialist German Day; they decorated their houses with flowers and displayed the national and city flags in honor of the numerous representatives. People came from Bavaria, Baden, Mannheim, Middle and Northern Germany, the occupied zones of the German-speaking parts of Austria; members of the Kampfverbände (Fighting Groups) were also represented. In order to channel the enormous influx of visitors, information centers were set up at the railroad station, and the Storm Troopers, assisted by the city police, saw to it that the groups marched in orderly fashion to their assigned quarters.

On the eve of German Day, Alfred Rosenberg published an official proclamation which set forth the main political and ideological themes of the rally. The text was printed in the *Völkischer Beobachter.* Rosenberg began by pointing out Nuremberg's historical significance. "German Day shall be our way of demonstrating our will and desire to change Nuremberg and make it again the center of national unity and defense, just as it used to be, and yet quite different."[1] He then discussed various points of National Socialist ideology:

Peace and quiet are not political ideals that are worth fighting for. Quite often peace and quiet are nothing more than laziness and mental atrophy. Not one nation has ever been saved with peace and quiet. On the contrary, nations have been destroyed and defeated by and through it. Order is of importance only when it shelters the adventurous life, never should it be a hindrance. . . .

State authority is only an abstract idea without foundation for the German men of today. The German heroes in the Ruhr and Middle Germany who saved the state's authority in Munich fought for the parliament of the Eberts and were thanked for their efforts with a kick. They were all upright soldierly men who had recognized their enemy. They could not understand that the battle could not be fought with hand grenades but with lies in the press, political schemes, and rulings of the parliament. Our Freikorps was not backed by an organized political movement and did not have the benefit of a prudent, politically understanding leader. This is the reason why the sacrifices of these heroes did not benefit the German people, the *Nationalgedanke* [National Idea] or the national movement struggling for freedom. It actually strengthened the position of the criminals of November 9 and the Jewish democrats in the stock exchange. The people of Nuremberg should realize finally that enthusiasm, militarism, and organizations as such are of no importance to the struggle for freedom of the national *Kampfbewegung*. It is just a waste of time as long as they are not fighting for a clearly defined German goal. We must stop the illusion that somewhere in our country today there exists a local government that is worth protecting, even with one man.

Rosenberg then accused the local governments in Germany of being strongly pro-Communist. He ended his proclamation with:

In Germany only German rights and German laws can be of value. National traitors should have their national rights revoked. German national rights should be enjoyed only by the men who protect Germany and her honor in our country and abroad. We have to draw our conclusions and discuss the consequences at the rally in Nuremberg. Do we want protection for the democracy of Bavaria? Do we want a Volkspartei? Do we demand changes without submitting new and better ideas?[2]

In this proclamation Rosenberg used the same demagogical device as Hitler to appeal to the people: nationalistic issues which would arouse patriotic pride. After stirring their emotions this way, he could easily persuade them with his mélange of half-truths and legal, moral, and political distortions.

As is the case for the first Party Day, the only available account of German Day is the one in the *Völkischer Beobachter*. The events are described there in glowing tones and in great detail. On the evening of August 31, the famous castle of Nuremberg was festively illuminated. The next day, the party extended its official welcome to all visitors. The National Socialist bands played concerts throughout the city. At the last moment, the German Defense Minister, Otto Gessler, had prohibited the participation of army bands. In the evening, the party members assembled in the large meeting halls of Nuremberg and in a hall in the Luitpoldhain.

At one of the meetings, Streicher spoke. In cynical tones he ridiculed a request to allow Jewish citizens to participate in the rally, and he described the development of the party in Nuremberg.

The second day of the rally opened at the Deutschherrenfeld with a religious ceremony and a memorial service for the dead of World War I. Since 7:00 A.M., the groups had marched on the field in a well-disciplined, military fashion. The arrival of the flag company from the Katholisches Hospiz, where flags had been stored overnight, was enthusiastically cheered.

According to the *Völkischer Beobachter,* the religious ceremony was a deeply moving event. A hymn from the Thirty Years' War, "Deutscher Notschrei," was sung to the melody of the "Niederländisches Dankgebet." A local teacher and a minister shared the pulpit. The minister spoke in a loud voice that could be heard all over the field. He called the Jews enemies and asked those participating in the ceremony to fight to free Germany. It was not the only time a priest was to act as a mouthpiece of Nazi doctrine; quite a number of the clergy were attracted by the National Socialist movement, and later, under the sponsorship of the party, a group of young ministers formed a secessionist church of their own, the German Christian Church.

After the traditional Bavarian prayer for soldiers going into battle had been said, the groups arranged for the parade through the city. Half the market square was roped off by the police to secure ample space for the honorary guests. The other half of the square was filled with soldiers and officers of the army and a large crowd of spectators. The honorary guests were chauffeured from the religious ceremony to the market square. They were Prince Ludwig Ferdinand; Generals Erich von Ludendorff, Hofer,

Merker, Kleinhans, and von Tutschek; Admiral Scheer; Lieutenant Colonel von Xylander; Major Fehn, the president of the national organization of German officers; Professor Bauer, the retired Minister of Justice; Dr. Roth; and Lieutenant Colonel Kriebl.

Hitler and Ludendorff had arrived shortly before the guests. Cheers and waving handkerchiefs announced the arrival of the first parade group. A squad of mounted policemen with their own band opened the parade. Two companies of Ulanen (Lancers), wearing their traditional uniform, followed on horseback. Then marched the groups of loyal party members, eight abreast. The Pfälzer Treubund (Palatine Federation of Loyalists), many student organizations in their traditional costumes, and various youth organizations marched in the parade. The marchers goose-stepped past the generals.

Next came the Storm Troopers with their standards. The parade of the SA lasted for more than half an hour. Standing beside Ludendorff, Hitler watched them march—a scene that was recorded on film. They were followed by the Reichsflagge (National Flag), a nationalist group that had sent many representatives to the parade. Captain Heiss, their leader, reviewed his marching men from his position beside General Ludendorff. Their first group was a section of cavalry on horseback. The organizations that followed the Reichsflagge were Wiking, Oberland, Bayrischer, and Reich. These groups had also sent many representatives.

The entire parade lasted more than two hours. About a dozen bands marched. The number of participants must have been at least 80,000, and about 70,000 of them were members of the fighting groups. Almost all the participants were in uniform, though the *Beobachter* claimed that a large number were industrial workers.

The crowds gave Hitler and Ludendorff an enthusiastic farewell. In the evening, patriotic ceremonies were staged in meeting halls, especially at the Ausstellungshalle. The exhibition hall was decorated with flags, and a huge golden swastika entwined with black, white, and red cloth was fastened below the big clock. Since most of the men wore uniforms or had been officers in the old army, the assembly had a military appearance. There were some technical difficulties, for the hall was utterly inadequate acoustically. Platforms for the speakers had been erected on both sides of the room, but only the people sitting near the rostrum were able to follow the speeches. According to Hitler's recollection of the meeting, there were 2,000 people crowded into the hall: "I also remember German Day in 1923 in Nuremberg. It was the first time I spoke in a hall that could hold 2,000 people. I had no experience as an orator. At the end of twenty minutes I was speechless."[3] Altogether Hitler made four speeches that evening and was enthusiastically cheered at each gathering.

Although opposition groups tried to interfere with the course of the activities, the meetings proceeded without major disturbances. Participants in the rally, however, were attacked by Communists; a flag bearer and two of his companions were assaulted by a large group of Communists in one of the streets, and some army officers were publicly molested. The Communists also denounced prominent personalities in the party over loudspeakers. Still, the departure of the participants at the end of the rally took on a festive atmosphere as they carried their banners to the station. Late in the evening, the Nuremberg castle was once again illuminated in their honor, and the citizens of Nuremberg showed up in large crowds to bid them farewell. The *Beobachter* report ends with glowing words about the patriotic sentiments expressed during the day.

The significance of this rally is probably best expressed in a proclamation drawn up by Hitler and two collaborators and published in the *Beobachter* on September 14, 1923. The first paragraphs restated familiar Nazi propaganda themes—Germany was a nation enslaved by foreign interests, the Versailles Treaty was unjust, the heavy hand of the enemy had to be shaken off. This was followed by a demand for freedom—a freedom which, according to the authors, the Weimar Republic could not grant because the republic was dependent on the enemy. The authors presented themselves as the only hope for this freedom: "The complete separation of our movement from the revolutionary government is the main premise for success. We are a national fighting group, not a political party. We are not engaged in party politics, but want to be fighters for Germany's freedom. We will fight anyone and anything that stands in our way."

The proclamation listed the enemies of the party: Marxism, Judaism, pacifism, the Weimar Republic, the parliamentary system and majority rule, and international capitalism. The authors pointed out the lack of a strong central government. Knowing the

Germans' love for their local ways, they promised a government
that would allow them to maintain the expression of their regional traits and customs. They did not conceal, however, what
form of government they had in mind: "The German people desire to have the state in the hands of a strong man." The proclamation postulated nationalization of the economy, but it assured the
individual of the sanctity of private property, and attacked the
control of the German state by foreign capital. Hitler introduced
as early as this one of his most successful reasons for regimentation
—that German citizenship implies an obligation. However, he reserved for the Nazi party the privilege of defining what these
duties were. Emphasis was placed on nationalistic education of the
German youth, based on Christian principles. In the earlier years
of the movement, Hitler referred frequently to Christianity, a
maneuver to win various religious groups over to his side.

The proclamation indicated that once power had been gained,
every medium of public communication—schools, theater, literature, press, art, film, radio—would be used for the state's purposes,
and the authors promised future state support to fighters for the
Nazi revolution, adding that a strong army would be necessary to
protect the revolution's achievements.

The rally held in Nuremberg in the fall of 1923 was a step forward in the development of the party as a strong political power.
Local right-wing groups were assimilated into the party. A revolutionary fighting group was formed in which representatives of different professions and classes were brought together, and this
group was regarded as a symbol of the new German Reich. Little
was added to party ideology; the favorite preoccupations—anti-
Semitism and extreme nationalism—were publicly rehashed. With
this meeting in Nuremberg, the rally as an effective propaganda
medium was well developed. The Nazis' demand for attention was
finding a growing response among the public.

3   THE WEIMAR RALLY
1926

It may seem strange that after organizing two congresses in 1923, the party did not hold a rally again for almost three years. The reason is that National Socialism entered a period of severe crisis after the September, 1923, rally. The ultimate goal of the proclamation issued for that rally was the overthrow of the Weimar Republic. The weeks immediately following the rally were laden with tension. Hitler later admitted that from the very beginning of the National Socialist movement he had been planning a *coup d'état*. At that time, he was more determined than ever to force the government to give in to his demands. He put 15,000 of his Storm Troopers on the alert to strike the moment he gave the order, and on the night of November 8, the *Putsch* was attempted. It failed because of lack of cooperation from the army. Hitler was tried and sentenced to five years' imprisonment.

The main lesson Hitler learned from the attempted *Putsch* was that legal means would have to be used for a final victory over the Weimar Republic. He cleverly made use of his setback by declaring November 9 a day of martyrdom when, according to him, heroic patriots had shed their blood for the liberation of their country. After he took power, the day was celebrated annually.

Hitler was actually quite unrestricted during his short prison term. Weber, Kriebl, and Hess served their terms at the same prison; they were allowed to see each other frequently, and Hitler had ample opportunity to dictate his book, *Mein Kampf*, to Hess and another assistant. During the nine months of Hitler's imprisonment the party was disbanded. When Hitler was released, in December, 1924, he at once began to reassemble his followers. His new start met with success, for in January, 1925, the ban on the party was lifted. Hitler regained permission to speak in public and to publish a National Socialist newspaper. (However, after his first public appearance, most of the German states again forbade him to speak.)

Due to the reviving prosperity of the country, the National Socialists obtained an extremely small vote in the spring elections of 1925. The Weimar Republic remained in power, with the aged Marshal von Hindenburg as the new president.

In 1926, the important Hitler Youth organization was founded. This group gradually regimented the entire youth of Germany, putting it at the unconditional disposal of the party. It was also at this time that Paul Josef Goebbels, who until now had held back his full support for Hitler, became a member of the party. He soon became one of the party's executive officers, and in November, 1926, became Gauleiter of Berlin.

In July, 1926, the party once again felt strong enough to hold a rally. The city of Weimar was chosen for the rally because Thuringia was one of the few states in which Hitler was still permitted to speak.[1] As at the previous two rallies, a party proclamation, composed by Hitler, appeared in the *Völkischer Beobachter* on the eve of the rally. In the opening paragraph, Hitler reviewed the critical years that had elapsed since the last rally in 1923. He then stated that a party rally was not the place for political discussions and policy changes; he wanted to shield the congress from any trace of parliamentary spirit. Its only purposes, he said, were mass demonstrations and a show of unity and strength. "The

Party Day is a congress of delegates with the purpose of giving new incentive to the movement."[2] It was already evident that Hitler did not want the NSDAP to join with the country's other political groups to discuss Germany's destiny. National Socialism did not want to discuss problems; it insisted on telling the nation what its destiny was going to be, and the Nazis reserved for themselves the right to bring about a new Germany—not according to the will of the people, but according to the National Socialist program.

The proclamation ended with some of the goals Hitler hoped to achieve on this Party Day. They were formulated, however, as was so often the case, in the vaguest terms: "Beginnings made or solutions found to a number of important questions in relation to the party."[3] He also said he anticipated eventual universal consent to the idea of National Socialism, and to the party as its representative. Finally, he hoped for a show of strength and discipline—the two virtues by which his party would reach its goals.

This third congress was as meticulously prepared as the congresses of 1923. A long list of rally regulations was published in the July 3 issue of the *Beobachter*. The participants were advised that the precise timetable for the program would be strictly enforced; that police regulations were to be followed unconditionally; that an information desk located close to the railroad station would provide maps with the locations of the various meeting halls clearly marked; that special guards would be provided to lead the arriving groups to their quarters; that rigid restrictions against smoking would be enforced in all meeting halls and mass living quarters. To subsidize the rally, each participant was obliged to purchase a Party Day medal, which cost fifty pfennigs.

In the July 4, weekend edition of the *Völkischer Beobachter,* Hermann Kriebl published an article that reflected the ideas that preoccupied the Nazis at that time. Kriebl complained that due to the stipulations of the Versailles Treaty, Germany was not allowed to have a strong army of her own. He suggested various possible substitutes for military training of German youth: the work of gymnastic groups all over the nation was encouraged as fostering comradeship, physical fitness, and a sense of teamwork. These sport clubs could easily be organized so as to train a great part of Germany's youth—an excellent supply for the army. Another suggestion was for initiation of compulsory labor service, which would have both economic and educational benefits: the young people would receive excellent training in various fields, be taught loyalty to the nation by working together, and overcome their sense of class differences. They would not have to be paid, and great labor projects such as irrigation of swamps, road construction, and the cultivation of waste land could be undertaken at extremely low cost.

As in former years, the edition of the *Völkischer Beobachter* published the day after the rally gave a detailed summary of the proceedings. If one strips these reports of propaganda and pathos, enough information remains to reconstruct the actual events of the day.

At 10:00 P.M. on Saturday, July 3, the eve of the rally, a special train carrying party members from Bavaria arrived in Weimar. (The *Völkischer Beobachter* reported that enthusiastic demonstrations had been staged at every station along the train's route.) On their arrival, the 2,000 party members, dressed in shorts, marched through the city to the various meeting halls, where they were welcomed by the Thuringian party leadership. Arthur Dinter, district leader of Thuringia, with his assistants Ernst Ziegler and Fritz Sauckel, was in charge of preparations for the congress.

Reveille at 6:00 A.M. initiated the activities of the following day. At 7:00 A.M., the SA and SS assembled in the German National Theater for the ceremony of the consecration of the banners.

The national congress of the delegates from all parts of Germany was also held in the German National Theater. Every seat in the house was filled. Dr. Dinter opened the congress on behalf of the leadership of the party. Gottfried Feder, a prominent economist, then addressed the delegates. In his speech on the relationship between the state and the economy, he pointed out that Germany was in a very serious situation economically. As usual, Germany's economic plight was blamed on the Versailles Treaty, the Jews, the Weimar Republic, and the "stab in the back"—the betrayal of the German soldiers in 1918 by the crumbling home front. The high financiers were held responsible for the present inflation. Feder lashed out at the Reichstag, calling its members slaves of international capitalism. After hurling invectives at the other political parties, he ridiculed one of the sound principles of the Weimar Republic: "All a government's powers originate

with the people of a nation." Feder commented that merely to
count votes is complete madness, that experts have to make the
decisions, not a mass of people who do not understand the issues.
Here again, at this early stage, the future dictatorship is apparent.
It is difficult to understand how speeches such as this, which implied the worthlessness of free elections, which denied both the
ability and the right of the people to determine their destiny,
could win those very people's acclaim.

The financial secretary then gave his report to the congress. He
spoke of the financial difficulties with which the party had
been faced since November, 1923, when the party's funds had
been confiscated by the state and the party forbidden to collect
contributions at meetings.

Among other reports was one by Rosenberg, who discussed
the National Socialist press. He advocated that all party newspapers carry on their front pages the party insignia—an eagle and a
swastika in a circle of oak leaves. He suggested strict control of the
National Socialist press through a central party organ, which
would have the right to grant or withdraw a newspaper's privilege
to print the party insignia.

In the afternoon, Goebbels addressed the congress of delegates
in the National Theater. His speech was brief; however, he set
down some of the principles that were to govern his famous propaganda machine. He emphatically rejected the use of high-pressure
techniques to win over the Marxist labor groups in the Ruhr
Valley. Instead, he advocated the effective use of mass media:
oratory, better newspapers used as political mouthpieces (he ex-
plicitly rejected the middle- or lower-class newspapers for propaganda purposes), and vivid and suggestive posters, which, he
pointed out, would have psychological value.

Hitler then addressed the congress and spoke on "politics,
ideas, and organization." In trying his hand at philosophy, he once
again revealed, if one had wanted to see, the true tendencies of
Nazism. The masses are irresponsible, he said. Man is usually concerned only with his instinctive needs for food, drink, love, and
the reproduction of his species. Therefore, it is the state's responsibility to preserve the race: this is one of the prime objectives of
politics. He went on to point out to his listeners that Germany
had lost her political power in the world, and also the desire to be

a great nation. He deplored that Germany, because of her economic plight, had lost great masses of people to other nations. He considered the discouraging of emigration to be a task of great importance. He then boasted that the history of Germany used to be the history of the world; but Germany had lost out in the contest with other nations for the possession of colonial territories. One of the main functions of National Socialism would be to revive the nationalist spirit in the Germans and to nourish their aspirations for greatness and for political and economic strength.

There were a number of new political resolutions drafted by the party congress concerning the rights of civil servants. These were read by Wilhelm Frick (Minister of the Interior under Hitler). On the one hand, they promised an improved administration under future National Socialist rule; on the other, they openly threatened racial discrimination and nationalistic bias.

We demand:

1. The maintenance of the civil service with constitutionally warranted rights.

2. The service of the so-called revolutionary civil servants will be discontinued, since they lack the required education and training, and since they have been appointed to their posts through political parties after the revolution.

3. Removal of all foreigners and Jews from official positions.

4. Rehiring of able staff members and disabled veterans who have been dismissed from their jobs.

5. Preference be given to social relief candidates and disabled veterans when official positions are filled.

6. The German National Railroad and its officials have to be taken back from the Dawes corruption and its international bank and market capital, and restored to free possession and the service of the Reich.

7. Protection of the National Post Office and other administrations of the state and agricultural regions from "Dawesation" and privatization.

8. Vigorous revision of salaries of civil servants, especially for minor positions; a basic minimum salary must be determined.

9. Providing inexpensive apartments and housing through nationally financed housing projects.

The old issue of the annexation of German-speaking territories outside the borders of Germany proper was again brought up, this time at a special meeting. A resolution was adopted that all Germans, inside and outside Germany, were eligible for party membership, provided they pledged full support to Hitler's fight for power. Those who lived abroad would be admitted to the party under the condition that they would work relentlessly for the eventual annexation of their territories to Germany.

Mass demonstrations were held in the afternoon and in the evening at various places throughout the city, and the 1926 Party Day came to a close.

Needless to say, Germany's uncommitted press did not report the events of the rallies as enthusiastically as did the *Völkischer Beobachter*. Their reactions ranged from indifference or faint curiosity to outright hostility. The *Vossische Zeitung* reported that "respected citizens and women" had been molested by Nazis in Weimar. The *Berliner Tageblatt* commented: "The 'elite' that Hitler and Dinter assembled with them in Weimar made the worst possible impression. One was able to note many unemployed workers who could not have been able to finance their trip to Weimar. They were penniless when they arrived at their destination. Their appearance was without dignity; they were noisy from morning to night on the streets and in a few restaurants, and terrorized the city." In its issue of July 4, the *Fränkische Zeitung* joined the chorus of warning and critical voices:

> As always at such national events, many unemployed workers were among the party members; their fare had to be paid for them. Some of the other members were also without funds, which was the natural reason for the many brawls in restaurants. For certain reasons it cannot be denied that 90 per cent of the participants at the rally were proletarians—laborers, employees, and unemployed workers. That it was not a gathering of the "elite" can be illustrated by the large number of incidents where police action was required. The local Reichsbanner group was wise in advising its members not to wear their party symbols on Saturday or Sunday to avoid unnecessary incidents. Nevertheless, a few men who were well-known republicans were insulted in most shocking ways.

These newspaper reports give a view of the rallies quite different from the enthusiastic accounts in the *Völkischer Beobachter*, which credited all participants with model behavior. It was during the 1926 rally that the *Völkischer Beobachter* took pains for the first time to warn its readers against the "Jewish-controlled press," as it called the critical, democratic newspapers.

The 1926 rally in Weimar was held during stormy times for the party, which had just emerged from one of its most severe crises without serious loss, but hardly stronger than before. The issues discussed during the meeting showed an unwavering belief that the future belonged to the Nazis, and an unchanged, primitive determination to achieve national control at all costs.

4   THE DAY OF AWAKENING
1927

The Weimar Republic was at the height of its popularity in 1926 and 1927, and the German people as a whole were not inclined to join extreme political movements. It may have been for this reason that the confident government again granted Hitler permission to speak publicly in Bavaria and Prussia. Yet despite this relative tranquillity, the membership of the National Socialist party rose from 17,000 in 1926 to 40,000 in 1927—an increase of more than 100 per cent in a single year. Therefore the Party Day of 1927 was more than a mere rally of loyal forces; it was the first massive demonstration of the National Socialist strength and solidarity as a political power. The party took great pride in its new status and in its history. The 1927 rally was considered the first significant Party Day.

From this year on, all official party congresses were held in Nuremberg. In 1927, the party did not yet have the grandiose edifices that were to provide the theatrical background for the rallies of the 1930's. The site chosen for the rally was a large, grassy field outside the city. It was known to Nurembergers as the Zeppelin-wiese (Zeppelin's meadow), because Count von Zeppelin had once landed his aircraft there. Another large, desolate area at the out-skirts of Nuremberg known as the Luitpoldhain was also used. In-door meetings were held at the Kulturvereinshaus in downtown Nuremberg. A suite of rooms in the hotel Deutscher Hof was taken over by the preparations committee for its operational head-quarters.*

The preparations for this congress were carried out with the efficiency that had already become traditional. Since 1923, Julius Streicher and Willy Liebel, Nuremberg's mayor, had been instru-mental in organizing the rallies; Viktor Lutze, later to become head of the SA, had been assisting in organizational work since 1926. This year, it took thirty men working around the clock for several weeks to handle the sleeping arrangements. Thirty-four mass sleeping quarters were ready to receive the arriving partici-pants; each was large enough to hold 5,000 men. For this rally, the railroads made increasing efforts to cooperate in accommo-dating party members. Nuremberg's director of the National Railroad reported officially that in the two days August 20–21, forty-seven special trains arrived at and left Nuremberg. From his statistics, we can deduce that approximately 160,000 people at-tended the rally.

The fact that a seat at a window along the marching route rented in advance for as much as twenty marks indicates the growing interest of the public in this party event. Yet not all the people of Nuremberg shared this interest. The proportion that left the city during these hectic days grew as high as 50 per cent in following years. Even party members and their families were known to have avoided Nuremberg at rally time. Jews who re-mained in the city were often imprisoned for the duration of the rally.

By August 19, more than 5,000 party members had arrived, in-cluding all the prominent leaders. Most of the first day was taken up by arrivals and preparatory arrangements. No demonstrations

---

* It is interesting to note that the Grand Hotel in Nuremberg refused to ac-commodate Hitler.

of any significance took place. This first day, as at succeeding rallies, seemed merely a prelude to the hectic events of the following days.

The congress began officially on August 20.[1] Gauleiter Adolf Wagner of Bavaria read Hitler's opening statement, as Hitler wished to save his voice for his long speeches at the mass meetings; all future rallies were opened in this way. The proclamation contained nothing that Hitler had not said before.

Dr. Frick then spoke to the congress; he voiced the usual complaints about capitalism and Judaism, blamed the problems of the Weimar Republic on its lack of leadership, and pointed to Hitler as the only man able to rid Germany of all her evils. He warned against the immediate seizure of power, and predicted that the party would have a long waiting period before it could take command. This appeal for moderation should not be mistaken for political wisdom on the part of the National Socialists; between 1924 and 1929, the party was at its lowest ebb, and the Nazis would have suffered catastrophic defeat had they tried another *coup d'état*.

Next, the Czechoslovak delegate, Jung, addressed the assembly and assured them of the loyalty of his countrymen. He was followed by Count Reventlow, who headed, with Albrecht von Graefe, the Deutsch-Völkische Freiheitspartei, the extreme right-wing faction of the party at the time. He spoke on what he called "the dishonesty of German foreign policy." He accused three prominent politicians of deliberately lying to the nation in matters of domestic politics and charged that since the Versailles Treaty, the German government had slavishly followed the dictates of the Allies. He further blamed the present German leaders for having sold the German economy into slavery by involving it with the Morgan banking interests. With the Dawes Laws, Germany had lost control over its railroads, banks, and customs department, the income of which was going to international banking concerns. The count insinuated that if the Reichstag had had any decency, it would never have allowed this. According to him, Stresemann expected that there would be no significant changes on Germany's eastern borders, but the English overruled him. He charged that at Locarno Stresemann had silently agreed to surrender Alsace-Lorraine to the French and declare the Rhineland an international zone. Count Reventlow maintained that after signing the Versailles Treaty, which disarmed Germany, France began preparations for war by building a defense wall from Calais to Basel. He said that the slogan of the League of Nations—"let's scrap the artillery"—applied only to the scrapping of German cannons. He then laid down three demands that were to become later Nazi policy.

1. Neutral nations should investigate who was really responsible for the World War.

2. Germany should resign from the League of Nations.

3. Germany should change her international policies and stop imitating France. France was Germany's deadly enemy. Germany destroyed herself by imitating her foes. Any enemy of France was an ally of Germany.

Count Reventlow ended his speech by appealing to the German feeling for tradition: National Socialist policy, he claimed, would follow in the footsteps of Bismarck.

Gottfried Feder then reported on the state of the economy as the Nazis viewed it at that time. He claimed that while the German nation had to make the highest sacrifices to pay its war debts, industrialists and financiers gained huge profits. Once again the anti-Semitic note was heard: according to Feder, 90 per cent of the financially successful men in Germany at that time were Jews. He described the fluctuation of the stock market: setting the average value of each stock at 100 per cent in 1923, they had dropped to 60 per cent in 1924 and risen to 300 per cent in 1926— the value of the stocks fell and then rose steadily—although there was no change in the national economy.

On the evening of the second day, the SA assembled on the outskirts of the city to prepare for a torchlight parade. According to the *Völkischer Beobachter,* thousands of people were waiting outside the hotel Deutscher Hof, where Hitler was to review the parade from the balcony of his suite. As each SA man passed Hitler, he raised his torch in salute.

On the third and last day of the rally, the SA massed early in the morning in the Luitpoldhain for the consecration of the flags. Huge torches illuminated the morning sky. After Hitler and the other party leaders arrived, the party flags were carried to the grandstand, where they provided an effective background for the

ceremony. According to the *Beobachter,* thousands of spectators
came to see the consecration of the flags. In his consecration address,
Hitler reviewed the history of the movement and of the National
Socialist flag. He struck a startling note when he invoked God's
help for the party's success.

After the consecration ceremony, the spectators returned to the
city to watch the parade of the SA. The houses along the marching
route had been decorated with swastikas and flowers. The leaders
of the party and their families were assembled on the speakers'
platform. The windows overlooking the Hauptmarkt had been
rented to ardent sympathizers, and the policemen, in their blue
uniforms, had great difficulty controlling the excited crowds in
the streets. The SA band from Potsdam opened the parade at
11:00 A.M.; leading the first detachment was Adolph Hitler. As
each marching group approached the reviewing stand, the party
leaders stepped to the front of the platform to salute. All 30,000
members of the SA were in the parade; they marched in companies, battalions, and regiments. Each group was led by its own
band and carried its own flag. According to the *Beobachter,* spectators handed the marchers flowers. As the SS formations came by,
the crowd burst into spontaneous cheers. Enthusiasm grew until
spectators finally broke into the national anthem. The parade
lasted more than two hours.

The last official event of the rally was the closing ceremony that
afternoon.[2] Alfred Rosenberg made the first speech. After ac-
knowledging the show of strength during the rally, he spoke about
Germany's lack of living space, a problem that was to play a great
part in the Nazis' claims to additional territories in the middle
and late 1930's. He declared it was the task of the party to provide living space for a hundred million Germans. He pointed out
that since the beginning of the nineteenth century, Germany's
sense of her national characteristics and national unity had di-
minished, and had been influenced by economic groups that had
their centers in London, Paris, and New York. He deplored the
fact that the big financial interests were overruling national interests; the reason, he said, was that the great banks of the world
were dominated by Jews, who had never had a country of their
own and therefore had no regard for national considerations. He
drew a crude caricature of the banker, in black clothes and gold-
rimmed glasses. He said that American high finance was com-

pletely dominated by Jews; the American banking system, which comprised 30,000 banks, was founded by a German Jew, Paul Warburg. He gave statistics on the amounts of loans and interests earned by these banks. In London, he said, international finances were steered by the Strauss brothers, Julius Klein, Bernard Baruch, and the Samuel family. Rosenberg claimed that Jewish-controlled high finance was attempting to form an international world state by means of merger and the uniting of powerful capitalistic combines; in this way, any sense of national character-istics, race, and individuality would be wiped out. He credited the Italian Fascists with being the first to fight against the institution of this utopian world state. The large banking institutions, the international press, Freemasonry, B'nai B'rith, the League of Na-tions, and Marxism were described as the means whereby the capitalistic rulers worked. He called for a world-wide anti-Semitic front to combat the world organization of the Jews.

Rosenberg then returned to the Italo-German relationship. Italy, he said, had problems similar to Germany's. Both countries were overpopulated, and Italy's young people also emigrated. France, Rosenberg accused, was preparing for war against Italy as well as Germany. (It is interesting to note that while the Nazis were calling for a merger between the Italian Fascists and the German National Socialists, in order to create a power to counterbalance "international capitalism," Mussolini and his party hardly knew of Hitler, and those who did thought very little of him.)

After Alfred Rosenberg, Dr. Dinter made a speech which out-lined, for the first time, a systematic anti-Semitic doctrine that anticipated the Nuremberg Laws of 1935. He opened his attack on the Jews by equating Judaism with materialism. Aryans were por-trayed as the exponents of idealism. Dinter argued that "racial chaos" is the consequence of materialism. The Jews, he said, lacked a sense of racial purity, and were capable only of bringing about destruction. This supposedly explained why the Jews, who were described as parasites by nature, had never had a country of their own. He then proceeded to cite biological "laws" according to which "Jewish character" persisted for generations, even after many mixed marriages. Dinter deplored the fact that more than 3,000 titled families had lost the purity of their blood through marriages with Jews. He called for strong laws preventing marriage and even friendship with the "Jewish race," for otherwise, within a few decades, the Aryan race would be a thing of the past. He then offered a number of suggestions to curb the Jewish influence:

1. Judaism should be banned in Germany and the Jews' German citizenship should be revoked, making their influence, as non-citizens, minimal.

2. Jews should not have the right to be elected to government posts, nor should they be allowed to teach or be judges.

3. Laws should be passed to forbid marriages of Jews with Aryans. A Jew having intimate relations with a non-Jew should be hanged.

4. Jews should not be allowed to buy property in Germany.

5. All Jews who settled in Germany after 1914 should be expelled, and their properties confiscated.

These five points, he claimed, could be the beginning of a solution to the "Jewish problem" in Germany.

Goebbels followed Dinter with one of his routine speeches on the value of propaganda in politics.

At a special meeting of the finance committee, it had been decided to ask each party member to contribute two marks to the party's campaign fund for the coming elections. After this decision had been approved, Hitler addressed the meeting. He stressed the need for a greater number of participants in the next rally and urged the members to work ceaselessly for the party's cause when they returned to their homes. Funds were needed, he said, to meet the costs of the rally, and although the participants had already been heavily taxed by paying their train fare and purchasing torches for the parade, he would welcome further contributions from those members who were financially comfortable. Thereupon, he and the other leaders took off their hats and went among the assembly to take up a collection.

Hitler closed the congress with a long speech—the only one he made during the rally. He discussed the lack of living space, which had increasingly plagued Germany since the end of the war. He emphatically ruled out the possibility of a solution through the reduction of the birth rate, since the party wanted a nation rich in manpower. He suggested as the ideal solution the peaceful distribution of land according to the rate of population. The rest of the speech was a confused mixture of demands for a population increase and purity of the race, and tirades against majority rule.

Opinions seem to have been divided as to the success of the 1927 Party Day. Stephen H. Roberts relates the following impressions:

The third Parteitag was held in Nuremberg in August 1927, but was not a great success. The city remained comparatively empty. I went there during the three of its meetings, and easily found accommodations, in the ordinary way. The townsfolk did not take it seriously. They enjoyed the torchlight procession—that was all. Hitler blessed twelve new standards and took the salute of 30,000 brownshirts in the Town Square, but not even the appearance of the banned Berlin formations or their subsequent altercations with the police could arouse much enthusiasm. Indeed, the gathering was so dismal and the people were so bored by Rosenberg's cultural campaign that it was resolved not to hold a congress in the following year.[3]

The press gave more attention to this meeting than in previous years. The *Münchener Post* wrote: "The citizens of Nuremberg are happy to have the party day of the NSDAP behind them. The affair lasted for three days. The working people reacted very coolly to the Wilhelminian megalomania of the party members. The parade and review were merely a final demonstration to salvage some of the prestige."

The *Bayrischer Kurier* of August 24 commented:

Only a few thousand followers of Hitler, wearing uniforms and medals, attended the party day. It seemed to be only a small-scale demonstration in comparison with the demonstrations of Hitler's followers in the city of Nuremberg in the past. The reporter noticed especially that this so-called workers' party had very few workers as active members. Most of them were young office clerks and students. The majority of the members are still youths. The reason for this suspicious rejuvenation is that only romantic youngsters are able and willing to believe in the empty phrases of Hitler.

As far as can be ascertained, the Italian press for the first time commented favorably on a rally. The leading Italian newspaper, the *Corriere della Sera,* called National Socialism the most noteworthy strength of the new Germany.

The speeches were the most interesting feature of the 1927 rally. Dinter's anti-Semitic harangue must be taken as more than incidental agitation; it clearly foreshadowed the Nuremberg Laws of 1935. Other speeches foretold the German-Italian alliance of the late 1930's, and the withdrawal from the League of Nations in 1933. It will become increasingly evident that the party congresses can be read as a barometer indicating the changing climates of party doctrine.

5 THE PARTY DAY OF COMPOSURE
1929

The growing political success of the Weimar Republic on both the domestic and foreign fronts and the complete failure of the right-wing groups in the 1928 elections were severely damaging to the Nazi party. This decline in popularity is generally considered the reason no party congress was held in 1928—a year in which the Nazis took a spectacular beating at the polls. In 1928, the Social Democrats increased their vote from 7.8 million to 9 million, whereas the extreme right-wing German National Party dropped from 6.2 million to 4.3 million. The Nazis scraped together a meager 810,000 votes, which gave them 12 out of 491 seats in the Reichstag, making them the ninth party in size in the chamber.

The Weimar Republic—perennial butt of Hitler's political harangues, labeled by him a "Jew-ridden republic of betrayal," whose members had been branded as "November criminals"—

had scored one political victory after another. Stresemann had successfully negotiated a settlement of the reparations and ended the French occupation of the Ruhr; he had managed to restore law and order in the German cities, stabilized the currency after the critical years of inflation, and secured Germany's entrance into the League of Nations. These achievements robbed the Nazis and the other right-wing groups of their favorite arguments.

The economic situation, although it looked promising at first sight, was actually critical. The generous flow of money in the German economy was based on excessive borrowing encouraged through the Dawes Plan. The official estimate of Germany's foreign debts at the end of 1930 was between 28,500 and 30,000 million gold marks, all of which had been borrowed between 1924 and 1929. These loans had been obtained at extremely high rates and on very short notice. The money was spent quite extravagantly, and neither the government nor businessmen seemed concerned about their difficulties in meeting their financial obligations. This gave an air of instability and irresponsibility to the economic life of the Weimar Republic.

By the beginning of 1929, the tide very slowly began to turn in Hitler's favor, as he found supporters among the most influential members of Germany's big industry. By far his most powerful backer was Alfred Hugenberg, one-time director of the Krupp concern, who had made his personal fortune during the inflation and bought a propaganda empire with his profits. He built a great chain of newspapers and news agencies and held a controlling interest in the UFA, the leading film company in Germany. He became a leader of the German National Party. Other important political groups that went over to Hitler's camp were the Stahlhelm, the Pan-German League, and such powerful public figures as Albert Voegler, president of the United Steel Corporation, and Hjalmar Schacht, president of the German Reichsbank. All these groups and individuals were right-wing extremists whose political luck had run out with the elections of 1928. They supported Hitler not so much out of sympathy for the Nazi party as to use it for their own political purposes. It was largely through Hugenberg's propaganda machine that Hitler managed to gain power in Germany. As a result of this substantial support, the party was able to recover from its setbacks, and once again felt strong enough to hold another party congress.

That a change had taken place in the National Socialist Party could be seen in the program of the 1929 congress. There were to be great fireworks and a nocturnal motorcade through the town. The number of participants increased significantly: there were to be thirty-four new standards, 60,000 men, and 2,000 Hitler Youth. The ceremonies of this and future rallies were changed by the erection of a war memorial in honor of the dead of World War I. It had been built by the city of Nuremberg and completed late in 1927. The city did not intend to provide the Nazis with a setting for their annual ceremonies, but, as it turned out, this monument was to be the center of chauvinistic hero worship from this time on.

The National Socialist Party congress was opened at 11:00 A.M. on August 2 in the main hall of the Kulturvereinshaus. Hitler and other party leaders were seated at the president's table. Representative Gregor Strasser was the chairman. Fanfares announced the opening of the Party Day. Streicher welcomed the delegates, and Adolf Wagner read Hitler's opening statement. It was the same line Hitler had used for years and was to use until the very end of his career: he wrote of the injustice shown the German soldier by the home front during World War I, injustices to Germany by the other European nations after the war, and injustices to National Socialist Aryans, such as himself and his friends, by Communists, Social Democrats, and Jews.

The first speaker at the afternoon session was Gottfried Feder. His speech dealt with the financial restrictions imposed on Germany by the Allied powers. He discussed at length the so-called Young Plan,* which he claimed would make the Germans financial slaves. The economic vacuum thus forced on Germany for two generations would increase the flow of German emigrants to other nations. He pointed out that, at best, those Germans would be used as cannon fodder by the Allies for capitalistic interests in future wars. The national debt imposed on Germany, he claimed, had climbed to eighteen billion marks; he emphasized the determination of the NSDAP to fight the Young Plan and the dictatorship of the international stock market.

* So called after American banker Owen D. Young, who in the winter of 1929 headed a committee of experts determining the amount of Germany's future reparation payments. The Committee signed a report on June 7, 1929, which required Germany to pay reparations for fifty-nine years. The annual payments were fixed on a graded scale, the average of which was considerably lower than the sum already being paid under the Dawes Plan.

Dr. Goebbels then addressed the congress on "Propaganda as the Key to Political Power." He was followed by Rudolf Buttmann, who spoke on idealism as a creative force in politics.

According to the *Völkischer Beobachter,* there was an incident of violence on the following day: the wife of an SA man was fatally wounded in a gunfight with Reichsbannermen. One Reichsbannerman was also slightly wounded. The Berlin police were said to have sent three men to investigate the incident.

The highlight of August 3 was the fireworks display at night. A crowd estimated at 150,000 went out to the Stadium to watch it. As darkness fell, a brass band flanked by men carrying torches marched into the Stadium. The fireworks were the most impressive the city had ever seen. They were made by Sauer, a fireworks manufacturer, who designed the display with great craftsmanship and skill. As the finale, a swastika appeared in the evening sky, surrounded by a circle of green leaves and crowned by a huge eagle. Five bands accompanied the crowd as it sang the national anthem.

The first major event of the following day was a memorial celebration for the dead of World War I. The ceremony was on a grander scale than ever before. Formations of SA and SS assembled early in the morning in the Luitpold Arena. In front of the newly constructed War Memorial was a stone coffin topped by a helmet, and behind it stood a stone cross. The coffin was covered with hundreds of wreaths. After the bands played the "Niederländisches Dankgebet," Hitler arrived, accompanied by the SA leaders and the carriers of the standards and Hitler Youth banners. The flags were arranged in front of the War Memorial, where General von Epp greeted Hitler. Hitler, General von Epp, and SA leader Pfeffer then stepped up to the memorial.

Von Epp made a short speech commemorating the war dead. Then fanfares and cannon shots gave the signal for the highest leaders of the party, the SA, and the bearers of the flags and standards to advance on the huge field. The crowd cheered as the rows of flags were carried in front of the leaders, while the band played the "Präsentiermarsch," and twenty-five new standards and the eleven new storm flags were carried past Hitler. He touched each flag with the "blood flag," the party banner that had been carried by the SA during the Munich *Putsch,* and which was stained with the blood of men wounded in the street fighting. The masses repeated three times in chorus "Germany, Awaken," the campaign slogan of the Nazis in the early years. This "consecration" of the new banners became a permanent ritual in the gigantic rallies of the 1930's.

The Storm Troopers stood in military order and, after a trumpet call, were addressed by Hitler. This speech, like all of Hitler's speeches from now on, was full of the mannerisms and clichés which he had been developing and which were later often secretly ridiculed by the people. He retold the history of the party from the beginning to the present time and made his familiar observations about World War I, its causes, its course, and its end.

The *Völkischer Beobachter* described the military review in greater detail than ever before. To the rhythm of Prussian military marches, the columns of SA men began to march by the leaders. The parade was led by groups representing the eastern provinces of Germany. They were followed by delegates from northern Germany and the middle and southern provinces. Participation in the parade was so great that it took the delegates from southern Germany one hour to march by. An unusually large contingent of Hitler Youths also marched. The delegates from the Palatian, in their white shirts, drew particularly loud applause from the watching crowd, since the French had forbidden them to wear the brown Nazi garb. The groups from Saxony and Bavaria were estimated at 10,000 each. The foreign representation was greater than ever before. Delegates from North and South America, the Sudetenland, South Africa, Sweden, and Austria attended the parade. The SS made up the final columns. It took the 60,000 participants in the parade four hours to march by the reviewing stands.

At 5:00 P.M., a large meeting took place in the Kulturvereinshaus. The first speaker was Alfred Rosenberg. He told his listeners that the formative years of the movement were behind them, the ground work had been done, but the great task of creating a giant national organization still lay ahead. He again attacked democracy and liberalism, and charged that they turned nations into masses of unrelated individuals with no political unity. He also reproached Marxism for having poisoned nationalism in the nineteenth century; this was all the more painful, since Nazi ideology saw nationalism and socialism closely and vitally linked together. "Our definition of socialism is measures taken by the state to protect the nation as a whole against all exploitation and individuals against private profiteers." He explained that the character of National Socialism was directly opposed to that of Marxism and Liberalism.

> We are against internationalism, which destroys the foundations of the ability to think and to feel. We are opposed to the struggle of the classes, which stirs up organizations and groups to revolt against each other. We are against pacifism. We are also against the idea of robbing individuals of their personal property. We strongly believe in our moral right to our private property. Our party offers the most effective protection of these rights.[1]

These observations are interesting, since Rosenberg here clearly draws a dividing line between the goals of Communism and National Socialism. The accent, at this stage, seems to lie heavily on realizing nationalistic interests—which means, of necessity, aggression whenever they are opposed; this reinforces one of Hitler's earlier statements, according to which every non-German is a potential enemy of Germany. This position proves that National Socialism was not genuinely revolutionary: it compromised the century-old postulate of the struggle between the classes, was soft on private capital, etc.

The next speaker was Fowgard, the delegate of the Swedish fascist party. He wanted, he said, to correct a misunderstanding. The fact that National Socialism had followers in other European nations did not mean that the party planned a United States of Europe. He pointed out that there was, however, a common bond between Sweden and Germany: both belonged to the Nordic race. He pledged Sweden's cooperation in the struggle between the spirit of the North and the spirit of the West—in other words, the common interest of the Aryans against that of democracy and Judaism.

Konstantin Hierl was the principal speaker at the congress that afternoon. He discussed the basis of German defense policies, saying the National Socialists believed that the state is the power that inspires a nation to fight for its existence.

> War is an act of power which tries to force the enemy to accept our will, and there is no limit to the use of that power. War is forceful politics, which will use all the military power available. Pacifism de-

nies the right of war as the last resort to settle differences and suggests a peaceful settlement through impartial references. But, as has been proved many times, the only way to settle differences is the natural right of each nation to show its superior strength. There is only one neutral judgment nations will accept, and that is historic achievements.[2]

He then disputed the common belief that the development of modern weapons, such as bombs and chemicals, would prevent a second world war.

The weapons that are available to any nation at any given time, no matter whether they are clubs, spears, guns, or airplanes, have never been the reason for the beginning or the postponement of a war. Furthermore, an effective defense against each new weapon was soon developed. As long as free nations exist that are willing to work toward their political goals, only war will be able to achieve the ultimate political aim.[3]

He distinguished between two kinds of pacifism, genuine and fake. If pacifism is genuine, it is because the nation is misinformed or misguided; if it is fake, it is a hypocritical display by a nation secretly preparing for war. He then gave his views on peace conferences: "Whenever big conferences are held to achieve everlasting peace and disarmament of the world, the world is getting ready for one of its big wars." He pointed out the importance of political leaders in future wars; statesmen, he maintained, would have to be military leaders at the same time. Hierl demanded compulsory military service for every German and the confiscation of private property by the state in time of war. He also took issue with the view of military experts that superior military equipment decided the great battles of World War I.

Since trucks had already begun to line up in order to begin transporting contingents of the SA back to their home towns, the gardens of the Kulturvereinshaus were closed to the public. The crowds that had gathered in front of the place were entertained by several SA bands.

Small incidents continued to mar the Party Days. On August 5, at a dark street corner, a group of SA men arrested a man who had attempted to knife one of their companions in the back and turned him over to the local police. On another day, a party member was shot and killed by a sniper. When a group of SA men wanted to search the houses in that area, they were prevented from doing so by the police. Another party member was attacked and stabbed by a group of men; he died later in the hospital. Later on, the Nazis complained that the opposition press had reported only the violence that had occurred during these days and had given little coverage to the rally itself.

These incidents obviously created great tension and fear among the participants; there are indications that the local police became increasingly nervous and feared more outbreaks of violence. When Hitler gave his final address at the end of the congress, the atmosphere must have been tense indeed, for he referred to the incidents and advised his followers to avoid attracting the attention of the police.

On the evening of August 5, Hitler closed the congress with a final address. His main theme was the deterioration of German national power. He pointed out that the Spartans secured their strength by rigorously selecting the strong and developing a healthy society. In his view, the opposite had happened in postwar Germany. Because of the nation's economic disaster, hundreds of thousands of Germans emigrated annually to other nations. Because America had a law that allowed only healthy and able-bodied men to enter it as emigrants, the weak and disabled stayed in Germany while the strong went to America. He demanded that a powerful government work for the increase of each individual's strength; he called for a new Germany that would be strong physically as well as economically. Under the present government, this once mighty nation had become a stale tourist country, "like our little neighbor Switzerland."

Commentaries upon the success of the 1929 rally differ. Ernst Hanfstaengl relates the following impression: "I remember being quite impressed by the marching and the bands at the rally, but of course it had not in any way acquired the mammoth Hollywood proportions that were soon to make it such an effective propaganda weapon."[4] Stephen H. Roberts' remarks were even more negative:

Numerous bloody clashes with the Communists gave added interest to the fourth Parteitag held at Nuremberg in August 1929, but failure lurked behind the proceedings. The speeches were dull. A new

Legal Association was formed and there was much discussion of the methods by which future leaders were to be trained. But the chiefs were too concerned with making a bid for actual power in some favorable state like Thuringia to trouble about the formalities of the congress.[5]

Nevertheless, this last rally of the 1920's was the largest congress of the National Socialist Party so far. It marked the end of the years of revolution, anti-government action, and petty fighting for power. The increased occurrence of violence foreshadowed the fierce battles of the future. The cynical denunciation of peace policies and the blunt praise of aggression and war to achieve national power forecast the frightening years to come.

6   THE SETTING OF THE STAGE

With the great world depression of the early 1930's, the Nazis emerged as the major political power in Germany. As the struggle for national control deepened, it became more and more apparent that the party would sooner or later triumph. With the appointment of Hitler as Chancellor in 1933, the National Socialists achieved supreme power in Germany, and henceforth the rallies grew from mere party gatherings into national events of great significance. Hitler therefore decided to build a gigantic stage on the outskirts of Nuremberg for the future party congresses.

He envisioned large-scale re-landscaping of the area around the Luitpoldhain and the Zeppelinwiese, which had already been used for the rallies of the 1920's. The plans were to create huge areas for mass demonstrations and parades—stadiums for the rallies of individual party organizations, a vast Congress Hall for indoor meetings, massive granite podiums for the speakers, and gigantic boulevards for show parades. The party also intended to provide accommodations for the press and the other visitors in the vicinity of the parade grounds. Long-range plans were even more grandiose: ultimately the whole city of Nuremberg was to be converted into a congress city, connected with the parade grounds by a single wide avenue. Work on these projects was conducted with increasing intensity until 1939, when the outbreak of World War II canceled all these activities except for the construction of the main Congress Hall, which was continued, with interruptions, until the winter of 1942–43.

The National Socialists undoubtedly knew that the creation of an area dedicated solely to ceremony and pageantry had precedents in world history. They knew that whenever a cultic tradition grew up in a nation, a proper ceremonial background emerged simultaneously with it; since the National Socialists liked to think of themselves in historical terms—for instance, announcing the beginning of the thousand-year Third Reich—they proceeded to fabricate history and tradition. They invented a cult overnight, and rather than let it grow naturally with time and tradition, they provided a ceremonial background through a gigantic crash program of construction. They wanted to display their power with pomp and circumstance, and borrowed theatrics from the great states of the past. The formidable, despotic might of the Pharaonic state of ancient Egypt was expressed in colossal temples and pyramids; Greece and Rome inscribed the omnipotence of the state in temples, palaces, monuments, and highways; Napoleon celebrated his triumphs in lavish buildings and monuments that changed the face of Paris. Hitler considered himself the equal of the great rulers of the past and did not hesitate to imitate their splendid gestures. From the very beginning, the highest priority was given to the construction of these parade grounds, and a maximum effort was made by large numbers of laborers, who worked almost around the clock between the summer of 1933 and autumn, 1939, to manifest the grandiose ambitions of the Nazi leadership. One positive result of these vast projects was the reduction of unemployment; work was provided for thousands of laborers of all professions. The projected März-feld project, for instance, was so vast that the preparation of the 510,000 cubic feet of stone that were to be used for this one site would have required 4.2 million hours of labor.[1]

When the National Socialists first chose the outskirts of Nuremberg for their mass meetings, the Luitpoldhain was a desolate area used for the storage of tram cars. Nearby was a large lot where the city built a sports stadium between 1923 and 1928. Another neighboring area was the Zeppelinwiese. In the middle of the nineteenth century, this area was a forest; destroyed by fire, it was used as a city dump for many years. Before World War I, when food became scarce, it was cultivated by farmers. After World War I, the city bought the land and converted it into a public picnic area.[2] In 1906, on the occasion of an industrial exhibition, the city had erected a pavilion near the Zeppelinwiese, a steel construction with large windows and skylights which was later used as a warehouse. After 1933, the National Socialists used the building for indoor meetings; they called it the Congress Hall.[3]

The Luitpoldhain was the first area the Nazis chose for their meetings in the 1920's. After they had seized power, it was the first site they developed for the Party Day of Victory in September, 1933. The *Völkischer Beobachter* of August 30, 1933, reported that during the previous two weeks a huge wooden grandstand had been erected, surrounded by three wooden towers ninety-six feet high and visible from a great distance. Large flags, seventy-eight by eighteen feet in size, were mounted on top of each tower. The flagpoles put up in this area stood 105 feet high. The speaker's platform and grandstands for 60,000 people were completed. The former was eighteen feet high and could accommodate 1,000 honorary guests. On one side of the field stood a large stand for the press that seated 1,500. Eighty-two loudspeakers had been installed. This work was done by 1,500 workers in a very short period of time. Hitler informed himself personally on the progress of the work. On August 19, he visited the Luitpoldhain and studied the blueprints of the grandstand and the War Memorial.[4]

The first large-scale construction on permanent installations was begun in preparation for the 1934 party congress. A contingent of 620 men was put to work to erect two gigantic concrete reviewing stands, each 500 feet in length. On the rally ground, six square miles in size, 270,000 cubic feet of earth had to be supplied to provide a solid base for a grass lawn that was to cover the entire parade grounds. The speaker's stand was eighteen feet high and was connected on both sides to special stands for the press. The entire structure was flanked by two huge stone towers, which were topped by the party eagles. These emblems of the party, designed by architect Kurt Schmidt-Ehmer, were nineteen feet high and had a wingspread of twenty-three feet. They had been built in sections, in a movie studio, and then shipped to Nuremberg in five trucks and assembled. In 1935, the eagles were replaced by others of more solid material.

In the background of this impressive stage stood four metal flagpoles 130 feet high.[5] By 1937, the construction work on the Luitpold Arena was almost completed. The grass plain in front of the new main grandstand was covered with large stone slabs. Ultimately the street that led into the area, as well as the avenue that led to the War Memorial, was paved with granite, transforming the entire Luitpold Arena into a great stone edifice.[6] Now the area extended over five square miles and could accommodate 150,000 participants and 50,000 spectators. The granite path connecting the War Memorial and the grandstand was 54 feet wide and 720 feet long.[7]

As early as 1929, the Luitpoldhain had proved too small to accommodate the constantly increasing number of participants, so the decision was made to use one or more of the adjacent fields for larger demonstrations. A number of stands capable of seating 350,000 spectators were set up on the Zeppelinwiese for the congress of 1933.[8] In 1934, a railroad station was built near the Zeppelinwiese to facilitate the movement of traffic to and from the rally area. The first large-scale construction on this site was begun for the rally of 1935; the work on this project was completed for the 1936 party congress. At this time, the field was expanded considerably to provide more space for armed-forces maneuvers and the meetings of the political leaders. A neighboring sports field and several tennis courts were demolished, and their space incorporated in the Zeppelinwiese; this enlarged it by a third and increased its capacity to 400,000 people. (The population of the town of Nuremberg was then 420,000.) On the far side of the field an avenue seventy-two feet wide was built, leading into the grounds; it was used for parades of political leaders and the armed forces.[9]

On Hitler's orders, a new main grandstand, sixty feet high, was built on the northeast side of the field. In the center was the speaker's platform. The back of the tribune and the steps leading to the honor stands for special guests were temporarily made out of wood. The grandstand was also to be completed by 1936, and to

be built entirely of brick and faced with stone tiles. At the back of
the grandstand stood iron scaffolding 120 feet high, topped by a
huge eagle and several large flags.[10] Another huge eagle was installed before the rally of 1935; mounted on eight vertical poles, it
was dismantled after the rally and replaced by a swastika.[11]

The principal building was erected for the Party Day of 1936. It
was a colossal new grandstand designed in neoclassic style. By
July, 1936, the back, which faced the street, had been covered
with marble tiles. The background of this imposing tribune was
formed by 170 stone pillars.[12] The actual parade grounds now
measured 960 by 870 feet, and were paved with stone to provide a
solid base for army maneuvers. Stone grandstands twenty feet high
enclosed the field on three sides. Thirty-four towers were evenly
distributed along these stands. Six flagmasts were mounted on
each tower.[13] Because of the party's great preoccupation with operatic effects, the lighting of the field was carefully arranged. One
hundred and fifty huge spotlights were installed to illuminate the
field for night ceremonies; they consumed 40,000 kilowatts of electricity during one evening. The Greek pillars in the background
were illuminated by 1,200 spotlights. An additional fifty powerful
klieg lights were placed strategically throughout the field to light
the grandstand, the speaker's platform, the flagpoles, and the field
itself. (At rally time, the illumination was so bright that the reflection in the sky could be seen as far away as Frankfort.)[14]

The finishing touches were put on the Zeppelinwiese in 1937.
The wooden benches in the grandstand were replaced by solid
stone seats. On the high stone walls that flanked the grandstand
pedestals were mounted that bore large metal bowls where open
fires were kept burning for the duration of the rally.

The stone floor in front of the grandstand was decorated with
tile mosaic. The necessary accommodations for the Red Cross and
post offices were provided at the beginning of the 1937 rally. At the
back of the grandstand a granite terrace was built, which was connected with the street level by a flight of steps.

Nearly 40,000 oak trees were planted around the Zeppelinwiese
to add some green to the stone surroundings. The oak tree was
selected because it was an ancient Germanic symbol of strength.

The almost blinding effect of the enormous white building was
achieved by the use of natural Jurassic limestone.[15] Folk humor
baptized the Zeppelinwiese *"Weisse Würstchen Wiese"* ("White

Sausage Field"), probably because of the row of white pillars behind the tribune.[16] This arena became the principal parade ground for the rallies of the 1930's, the largest and most imposing stage for the spectacle of Nazi power.

The last project to be completed before the war was the Congress Hall. Renovation of the old industrial exhibition hall was begun in preparation for the Party Day of 1933. The *art nouveau* façades were replaced by more sober rectangular walls, which were decorated with huge swastika banners. The indoor hall was 540 feet long, 150 feet wide, and 50 feet high. The estimated seating capacity was 20,000. The interior walls and the center posts were covered with fabric, and the posts were decorated with flowers. Seventy-six loudspeakers were distributed throughout the hall. There was room on the stage to seat 130 musicians. In addition, seats for 750 party functionaries were provided, and two side stands were reserved for the press. Forty-two spotlights, directed toward the ceiling, illuminated the hall. In 1935, an air-cooling system was installed along the ceiling. One of the largest electric organs ever built was set up behind the speaker's stand, with 4,000 pipes ranging from two to forty-eight feet in height. When neon tubes were first developed, in 1935, they immediately replaced the conventional ceiling lighting.[17] The chairs in the hall were hard, which made sitting through the long speeches extremely uncomfortable. Smoking was prohibited during sessions.[18]

The old Congress Hall was used for all indoor meetings during the rallies of the 1930's. At the 1935 rally, the cornerstone of a vast new Congress Hall was laid. The new Congress Hall was to be 670 feet wide, 870 feet long, and 150 feet high. It was to be 1.3 times the length and 1.7 times the width of the Roman Colosseum. The cost of construction was estimated at approximately $63 million.[19] The hall was to provide seats for 40,000 people and standing room for 8,000. The walls were to be decorated with 1,000 flags. The roof was to be supported by eighty-eight columns, each of them fifty-one feet high; the whole project would cover 160,000 square feet. The material for this building came from all parts of Germany. An extensive network of railroad tracks was laid around the whole site to facilitate the transportation of building materials,[20] and an estimated 150 railroad cars were used daily for shipments.[21] In 1935–36, a dam was built on the Dutzendteich, a large lake in the vicinity of the parade grounds, to keep the grounds dry.

With the outbreak of World War II, in 1939, work was stopped on all projects in Nuremberg except the new Congress Hall. It was Hitler's favorite project, and work on it continued until the winter of 1942–43. At this time, construction had to be halted because of the critical turn of the war situation. When work stopped, the building was approximately half completed. The roof, the second story, the interior construction, and the stage remained unfinished.[22]

Hitler had hoped to create a great sanctum with this building, a cultic center, a gigantic fascist temple, for the rally exercises—a pantheon of the German gods. Its colossal size expressed the Nazis' bombastic ideology and political ambitions, its hideous architecture inadvertently reflected its makers.

In 1936, construction was started on a wide parade avenue that was to connect the Märzfeld and the Luitpold Arena for the use of the armed forces and the Storm Troopers. The avenue was sixteen miles long and 240 feet wide, paved with granite blocks.[23] In August, 1939, it was reported to be almost finished.[24] The people of Nuremberg baptized the avenue *"Die Grosse Strasse"* ("The Big Street").[25]

Plans for still another large arena, intended to supplant the Zeppelinwiese, were made in 1936. It was also to be called the Märzfeld, and was to be used for parades of the armed forces. It would be a rectangle more than 2,100 by 2,700 feet,[26] surrounded by a stone wall and enclosed by twenty-six towers, each 120 feet high. The towers were to rise from the surrounding wall every 360 feet. The space between the towers was to be filled in by curtains of banners seventy-five feet high. The designer of the field was Professor Albert Speer, Hitler's favorite architect.[27] By 1938, the foundations of most of the towers had been laid, and in 1939, a great number of the towers were completed.[28] The stands would be able to accommodate 500,000 spectators.

In 1937, a fourth huge arena was begun—for future sports contests connected with the party rallies. It was located between the Luitpold Arena and the Märzfeld, and was also designed by Professor Speer. It was to be built in the shape of a horseshoe and to have a capacity of 310,000 spectators.[29] The cornerstone was laid during the rally of 1937; the building, like the new Congress Hall, was scheduled to be completed in 1943. The ground was broken in 1938; in 1939, most of the groundwork was finished, and railroad tracks for transporting building materials had been laid. In the middle of the construction area, a temporary tower was erected; it was to be the nerve center of the construction activities, from which the work could be supervised and directions given over a loudspeaker.[30] Work was stopped on this, along with all other projects in the parade grounds, at the outbreak of the war.

Long-range plans were made for elaborate hotel accommodations for the many party dignitaries and guests in Nuremberg. In the spring of 1938, work on a new press hotel was started, near the railroad station and the hotel Deutscher Hof. It was to be a five-story building with 285 rooms, a huge conference hall, a dining room, a beer garden, and a Bavarian-style balcony running the length of the hotel. During the party congresses, the hotel was to be reserved for reporters only, and would have its own post office and special telegraph and telephone facilities.[31]

Hitler and Hess always stayed at the Deutscher Hof; high party officials usually stayed at the Palmenhof. Underground passages between the hotels were dug out for easier communications between the party leaders and their staffs. Goering had especially luxurious quarters at the hotel Kaiserberg, which had been extensively renovated. Because of the elaborate electrical equipment installed there, a special room for switchboards had to be set up in the cellar.[32]

Thus the stage was set for the greatest spectacle of political fanaticism history has ever seen. The theatrical character of this whole gigantic stage can be seen in the careful arrangement of the actors' positions in the mass scenes. On the parade grounds, a system of markers was set up to indicate the exact locations of various groups and to ensure a symmetrical distribution of the 8,000 banners.[33] In an interview with press correspondents at the 1938 rally, Hitler announced that he ultimately wanted to create an entirely new congress city, built in the style of the future and connected with old Nuremberg by a wide avenue.[34] Although some of the biggest projects were interrupted by the outbreak of the war, and others took years to complete, the changes of scenery from rally to rally were like the changing background of a play from act to act. Even uncompleted, this project gives one a sense of the formidable totalitarian spirit that meant to mesmerize the whole nation with dramatic pageantry.

7   THE PARTY DAY OF VICTORY
1933

There were no official Party Days at Nuremberg between 1930 and 1933, for these were the years of the Nazis' concentrated efforts at achieving national power. The party more than doubled its popular support between 1930 and 1932, and in January, 1933, Hitler became Chancellor.

The conditions of the 1920's continued. Public disorder was widespread. Violent street fights became more and more a part of daily life in the major cities. One example was the case of Horst Wessel, a young Berlin SA leader who was shot and killed by the Communists. The furor over his assassination was cleverly manipulated by Goebbels to mold the young man into a party martyr and to swing public opinion in favor of the Nazis and against the Communists. Goebbels skillfully concealed the unsavory details of young Wessel's life and raised to the status of a national anthem a simple marching song that the young Storm Trooper had composed. It was sung at public meetings and used in the musical background at the Nuremberg rallies of the 1930's.

In the period between 1930 and 1932, the stability of the German government continued to deteriorate. The chancellorship of the Weimar Republic changed hands three times in 1932. The government was further weakened by Hitler's successful attempt to enlist the support of big industry. Due to his skillful tactics in a speech before the Industrial Club in Düsseldorf on January 27, 1932, he was able to convert many leading industrialists to his cause. He held the Weimar Republic responsible for the unemployment that drove millions of voters into the Communist camp. The Communist threat was obviously a persuasive argument to undermine the confidence of members of the Industrial Club in the government. Hitler pledged the full support of the NSDAP, if it should gain power, to uphold the privileges of private enterprise and to free the German economy of foreign domination.

Another decisive step in securing Hitler's position in this crucial period was his endorsement by the army, thanks to his strong appeal to right-wing nationalism and patriotism.

The NSDAP had its first decisive national victory when the nation went to the polls in September, 1930. Its vote grew from 810,000 to 6,409,600—a landslide that surprised even Hitler himself. He had hoped to increase his seats at the most to 50 or 60 in the Reichstag; instead, the Nazis gained 107. This spectacular success may have been due to the Germans' increasing dissatisfaction with a government that had failed to halt the deterioration of the economy. The continued growth of the party made it necessary to find a larger house for their headquarters. Hitler bought the old Harlow Palace in the Brienner Strasse in Munich; this mansion was redecorated and became the famous Brauhau. It remained the party headquarters until the end of the war.

The election campaigns of 1932 were conducted with the most modern techniques of mass persuasion—films, phonograph records, posters, and dramatic photography in illustrated magazines. The black magic of political slogans which the party developed in those years was never exceeded afterwards. Mass meetings were organized throughout the nation. Hitler traveled the entire nation by airplane, and the campaign was carried into the remotest rural constituencies. This gigantic effort of a highly organized propa-

ganda machine was unprecedented in the history of political parties, and explains to some extent why the Nazi vote showed a
marked increase in the years from 1930 to 1932. It rose from 18.3
per cent in September, 1930, to 37.3 per cent in July, 1932. Its
strength declined sharply in November, 1932, when 2 million of
the 13 million votes captured in July, 1932, were lost. In January,
1933, the party's luck changed again for the better. In the village
of Lippe it secured 39.6 per cent of the vote, an increase of 17 per
cent. Although this was only a local election, Nazi propaganda acclaimed the figure as a victory of national importance.

Aided by political intrigue and public dissatisfaction, Hitler
was appointed Chancellor on January 30, 1933. This was followed
by the systematic destruction of the democratic institutions in
Germany: the party seized control of the press and other mass
media, smashed the trade unions, disbanded all other political
parties, threw political enemies into concentration camps, and in-
stituted a new dark age of methodical, scientific torture and
murder.

To celebrate their rise to power, the National Socialists
planned to make the Party Day of 1933 the biggest ever. The
name of the congress, the Party Day of Victory, was suggested by
Hess.[1] The National Socialists used every possible facility to organize the coming rally. While the rallies of the 1920's had been
comparatively isolated party affairs, this year, for the first time, the
Party Day became a major national project. All the mass media of
Germany were employed to drown the nation in propaganda.

Since record attendance was expected, every square foot of sleeping room was reserved long in advance. All unused halls, restaurants, factories, and schools were to serve as mass sleeping quarters.
The SA, Hitler Youth, and Nationalsozialistische Betriebszellen
Organisation (National Socialist Organization of Local Party Cells)
were to sleep in tents on the camp ground.* The groups of SA

---

* An interesting and quite detailed description of these tent camps is to be
found in *The New York Times* coverage of the rally. The largest camp was adjacent to the Zeppelinwiese, where the men were housed in huge tents, each of
which could hold 400 men. On one side of the camp was a row of field kitchens.
These were twelve-foot-high brick constructions with huge ovens, and boilers that
produced countless gallons of soup. The camp for the 60,000 Hitler Youths was
similarly equipped, with 600 boys sleeping in a tent, in rows of ten tents. Each camp
was provided with its own fire department. (*The New York Times*, September 1,
1933.)

and SS that arrived in trucks were quartered in nearby villages.*
Two hundred and fifty special trains were requisitioned to bring
400,000 party members to Nuremberg. All sections of major highways going through the city were closed. After September 1, private cars were not allowed to enter Nuremberg; large parking
areas were made available at the outskirts of the city. During the
congress, planes were prohibited from flying over the city, so that
the noise of their motors would not disturb the speakers.[2]

Six hundred reporters were given special permission to attend
all the functions of the congress. Only 200 of these were foreign
correspondents;† the remainder were German journalists. An additional 3,000 reporters were registered to attend the Party Day,
but they had no access to the indoor meetings. The press headquarters, with immense working facilities and 200 soundproof
telephone booths,[3] was located next to the Congress Hall. The special guests who attended the congress watched the ceremonies
from the recently finished main grandstand. Numbering almost
one thousand, they included diplomats, representatives from
abroad, members of the Reichstag, high officers of the armed forces,
and Hitler's personal guests.[4] The foreign diplomats who attended
the rally traveled by rail to Nuremberg. Fourteen sleeping cars
were appropriated to transport them to the city; in order to save
hotel space, the diplomats lived in their sleeping cars during the
rally. The rally was attended by diplomats from Estonia, Denmark, Bolivia, Egypt, Haiti, Portugal, Mexico, Siam, Hungary,
Greece, Finland, Ireland, and the Dominican Republic.[5] For the
first time, a large contingent of Austrian SA men was among the
foreign visitors.

The 1933 rally had its official beginning with the arrival of Hitler shortly before 8:00 P.M. on August 31. He had come from

---

* The difficulties that had to be dealt with in finding quarters for the visitors
from all parts of Germany were not always organizational in nature. There were
many regional hostilities. For instance, the Bavarians were prejudiced against people from other provinces, especially the Prussians: "It must be pointed out that
the Bavarians have no love for the Westphalians; they call them 'bum-Prussians'
and usually treat them very coolly. But music overcomes all differences, and being
aware of that, we chose only Bavarian marches for that afternoon." (Report by an
eyewitness to the 1933 rally.)

† *The New York Times'* correspondent reported that a foreign journalist who arrived in Nuremberg was directed at the railroad station to his proper center. There
he handed in his identity card, was addressed in his own language by a uniformed
interpreter, assigned to a hotel room, and equipped with programs, a guide, and
every other convenience. (*The New York Times,* September 1, 1933.)

Munich with his cabinet and was cheered by the waiting crowd as
he was driven to the hotel Deutscher Hof. Later in the evening,
the city officials cordially greeted Hitler and the leaders of the
party at the Nuremberg Town Hall. Mayor Liebel delivered a welcoming address and presented Hitler with Dürer's engraving
"Knight, Death, and the Devil"—a fitting gift, since to the Romantics it represented Germanic knightly prowess in the face of
adversity and death. Hitler briefly answered the mayor's speech
and was driven back to the hotel.[6]

On the following morning, the congress was opened with great
pomp and ceremony. Hitler received a thunderous ovation from
the delegates, but, as usual, did not address the opening session of
the congress. After Hitler's arrival, the party banners were cere-
moniously carried into the Congress Hall and placed behind the
speaker's platform.

The session began with the overture to Hitler's favorite opera,
Wagner's *Die Meistersinger.* Then the whole convention rose and
sang the "Netherlands Hymn of Thanksgiving." This was followed by a piece of sinister pageantry: the blood flag was carried
by a steel-helmeted bearer to the front of the platform, and to the
throb of muffled drums, Ernst Roehm, chief of staff of the Storm
Troopers, read the roll of the party dead. It was a long roll, but
the large audience stood listening patiently and in silence.[*]

It was in this atmosphere that the presiding officer, Rudolf
Hess, began a very short opening address with the words: "I open
the Party Day of Victory." He said nothing that was new or no-
table. Following his address, a representative of the Italian Fascists, clad in black even to his long black gloves, was introduced.
He brought Mussolini's friendly greetings, and acknowledged the
welcome given to himself and his associates.

The high point of the session was Julius Streicher's reading of
Hitler's proclamation to the delegates. It set out to chastise the
scapegoat of the Nazis at that time—the influence of Marxism in
Germany. It credited the National Socialist movement with having overcome treason and perjury, and with restoring faith, honor,
and decency in Germany. After the seizure of power, the whole
nation had joined behind the National Socialist party to halt the

---

[*] *The New York Times'* correspondent expressed surprise and bewilderment at
the stern and ceremonious proceedings at this session, so unlike political gatherings
in the United States. (*The New York Times,* September 2, 1933.)

onslaught of Bolshevism in Germany. The proclamation offered
various vague suggestions for solving the nation's labor problems.
It attacked the usual targets of the Nazis—capitalism, foreign
domination, parliamentarianism, and the Jews. It called for the
future merger of the federal German states into one homogeneous
nation.

Later that same afternoon, Hitler spoke extemporaneously to
the League of German Culture and to a special group of invited
party leaders and diplomats. Outlining his very limited ideas of
culture, he once again unleashed a dull diatribe of warped racial
theories. He clearly indicated that non-Aryans should not expect
to be able to express themselves artistically in Germany in the future, and he emphasized the party's intention to keep music, art,
architecture, and all other artistic professions strictly Nordic.[7] He
once again asserted that the Jews had no creative talents of their
own.

On the following day, two outdoor spectacles were staged that
showed the Nazis' love and talent for massive theatrical effects.
The district leaders of the party assembled in the morning on the
Zeppelinwiese, and there was a huge review in which 160,000 high
party officials and their followers participated. The party leaders
stood in rows, divided by one wide middle avenue, with three narrow lanes on each side. In an impressive demonstration of mass
movement, waves of flag bearers came over the embankment in
the rear of the field; they swept through the blocks of men standing at attention, marching twelve abreast with their banners high
through the center avenue, and in single file through the narrow
lanes.

Hitler was greeted by his uniformed followers in the parade
ground and by 100,000 spectators in the stands with cheers that
reverberated throughout the arena. In his speech, he congratu-
lated the district leaders and the party as a whole upon their spectacular political victory and promised Nazi supremacy in Germany
for a thousand years to come.*

* An eyewitness has furnished interesting details about the gathering of the
formations in the field and about Hitler's appearance. "At 6:00 A.M. we had to leave
for the big meeting in the Stadium. We had to play for four hours from the
speaker's platform to entertain the assembling formations while they were waiting.
It was one of the most overwhelming sights to see from this high platform how
the vast Stadium filled slowly and very orderly with hundreds of thousands of
uniformed men and women. In the field itself, only uniformed groups assembled,
while huge crowds of civilians gathered on the side. Finally Hitler appeared with

A festive meeting of the Hitler Youth took place in the afternoon in the Youth Stadium. Sixty-thousand boys filled the arena to capacity. They had been especially chosen from the 1,500,000 members of the party's junior organizations and brought from all parts of Germany. They stood in long ranks; each boy carried a knapsack and a blanket roll on his shoulders, and a long knife with the inscription *"Blut und Ehre"* ("Blood and Honor") on the blade. The ritualistic parade of flags that had swept the Zeppelinwiese in the morning was repeated by these youngsters in the afternoon. When Hitler appeared, the enthusiastic greeting he received from his youthful followers lasted almost ten minutes before he could make himself heard.[8] When Hitler finally spoke to the gathering, his speech contained the same generalities as his address in the morning. He pointed out the responsibility of the youth to carry the spirit of this rally into their home towns and to their families.[9]

Later in the afternoon, the 15,000 district organizers, the hard core of the party's minor strategists, met in the old Congress Hall. The purpose of the meeting was to formulate solutions to three key problems: foreign relations, economic reorganization, and the racial question. It was intended that after official agreement had been reached, those attending the meeting were to carry these doctrines home and disseminate them in their constituencies.

The first speaker was Alfred Rosenberg, who spoke on the racial foundations of Nazi foreign policies. He pointed out that the party's greatest contribution was to the rebirth of nationalism. Socialism in Germany had betrayed the nationalistic cause because it was entangled with the international ideas of Communism. Rosenberg then elaborated in great detail his main theme: racial purity. He said that the party's greatest concern would be to keep the German race untainted. Only then would the nation be guaranteed to remain creative. He boasted that the leading German poets and philosophers came from pure Aryan stock. He emphasized that the National Socialists were not advocating racial hatred,

---

his staff. He sat down about six feet away from us. At this point I noticed the most interesting thing about this strange man. As he was sitting in front of us (it was by now about 9:00 A.M., and chilly rather than warm), I could see that Hitler began to sweat. He stared at the crowd which he could see but which could not see him yet. Slowly the back of his shirt began to discolor, a gradually growing dark spot began to show until his whole back was completely soaking wet. His apprehension seemed under control when he finally got up. We played the 'Crusaders' Fanfare,' and he began to address the crowds." (A report supplied to the author.)

but respect for the purity of the race. He decried the formidable influence of Jews on German society, but claimed that the party was not planning to persecute the Jews. It had, however, decided to fight for the restitution of elementary justice to German citizens. He continued: "We ask other nations: Is it to your interest to participate in a world boycott and political isolation of the German people . . . ?"[10] He said that Germany had saved not only herself but all Europe from Bolshevism, and that if other nations were to destroy the new Germany, the Communist peril would rise higher. The idea that Germany was Europe's sole defender against Bolshevism was used with great effect by the Nazis throughout the 1930's.

Gottfried Feder, who by this time had become Under Secretary of Economics, was the next speaker. He claimed that the present economic debacle was due to the fact that the unions and the professional groups were opposed to each other. He suggested that the remedy for the situation would be to encourage these groups to cooperate with each other.[11]

Feder was followed by Goebbels, who addressed the meeting on "The Racial Question and World Propaganda." He pointed out that the National Socialist revolution had successfully avoided bloodshed. He quoted Richard Wagner's malicious statement that the Jews are the demons of decadence and Aryans alone are creative. He claimed that the Nazi boycott of the Jews was motivated by the world-wide Jewish boycott of Germany. The persecution of Jews in Germany was denied. If people were harmed, it was for a good reason, and they should blame their fellow Jews abroad for anything that happened to them. He admitted that the Jews did not bear the sole responsibility for the present crisis in Germany, but he assured his audience of the party's intention to expose whatever role they had played in it. He then voiced the familiar complaint against "the Jewish penetration of the professions." He accused the Jews of having monopolized such fields as law, medicine, real estate, and the theater. He pointed to Germany's role as a bulwark against Communism: "The peoples who permit the Second and Third Internationals are conjuring up the very danger to themselves that we have just banned. The constantly progressing bolshevization of the economy, politics, and ethical life in its entirety is an open wound that, unless halted, will have the worst consequences."[12]

Goebbels ended his speech with a statement which, like so many the Nazis were to make in years to come, assumed an entirely different and frightening truth in the light of history: "We need not fear the verdict of the world in the racial problem, and in the solution of that problem lies the future of our people."[13]

The day's activities were crowned by a festive nighttime display of fireworks. Although an admission fee was charged, thousands of spectators came to see the sight. Despite the fact that the party organized such events in the most minute detail to avoid accidents, many injuries were caused by sparks that fell back onto the crowds. As many as fifty people were estimated to have been severely injured. Because of these incidents, increased precautions were taken at future rallies, and the immediate vicinity of the fireworks was roped off from the general public.[14]

At dawn on the last morning of the rally, members of the SA gathered for their final demonstration. Many of the groups met at their rendezvous as early as 3:00 A.M. Shortly before 8:00 A.M., the parade began to move toward the Luitpold Arena for the roll call and the traditional consecration of the banners. The ceremonial atmosphere reached its climax when, at 8:00 A.M., all the church bells of Nuremberg began to ring.

By 10:00 A.M., when Hitler arrived, the formations had assumed their positions. In the center of the field were 15,000 party flags; they seemed to dwarf the thirty-five flags of the visiting nations. For the first time, the Red Cross and the field hospital organizations were represented. Attendance was estimated at 150,000.

After Hitler had placed a wreath at the War Memorial, he briefly addressed the assembly. He assured his audience that Germany had not the slightest wish to win new laurels on the battlefield. No war, he declared, could bring her greater honor than she had won in World War I, in which she had held out against the entire world. The only dishonor in that war was brought upon the nation by the home front, and that shame had by now been wiped out.[15] (In fact, the party had frequently proclaimed that the only honor in this world was to be found on the battlefield, and that the only solution to Germany's present plight could be brought about by arms.) After the speech, the consecration of the new banners took place.

In the afternoon, the scene shifted to the beautiful town square of Nuremberg for the annual march past. Reviewing stands had been erected to accommodate approximately 10,000 spectators. A special section was reserved for the 100 oldest party members and their families and for the families of the 240 men who had been killed in the struggle for power. Standing in his car, Hitler reviewed the parade. Beside him was Ernst Roehm, the chief of staff of the SA. It was the last rally Roehm attended, for he was murdered in the purge of the following June. On the opposite side of the square three bands took turns accompanying the marchers. The houses surrounding the square were decorated with flowers and garlands, and spectators filled every window.

The parade was vividly described in *The New York Times:*

> Unceasingly and apparently tirelessly until almost dusk a stream of the well-knit, athletic youths chosen from 1,500,000 or more to come here for this demonstration passed, fading away down the street in a blare of brown caps and gray knapsacks. They moved by battalions, 500 strong and twelve men to the file. As the flags swept by, a forest of swastikas almost a block long for each regiment, every flagstaff was wreathed with the green oak leaves of victory and every man's cap bore a flower or a knot of green.
>
> Young Germany was showing its strength. And young Germany is very strong.[16]

Two hours later, Hitler closed the congress with a speech in which he expounded his theory of racial leadership. He made three points: a race should be kept pure because it was determined through a selective process; the same process should be applied to the leadership; democracy had failed because it failed to respect that process. People had different strengths and abilities, and this should be recognized in political life. The "higher" races had helped the world more than the "lower" ones. Only those best qualified should administer the state. The political leadership should be selected from among those people whose ancestors had created the nation. German decadence was due to the fact that a "foreign race" had introduced "false ideas" among the people.[17]

The New York Times' correspondent reported boycotts of Jewish-owned stores in the wake of the rally. Storm Troopers and other party members stood in front of shops and warned prospective customers that the owners were Jewish; force was seldom necessary, for people were too frightened to go inside. "The ordinary Nuremberg citizen has no anti-Semitic prejudices and wants to patronize the Jewish stores," the correspondent wrote, "but the amount of intimidation in the city, already great before the rally, is now enormously increased. . . ."[18]

For the first time, the press, now government controlled, gave the rally full coverage. For days before and after the rally, the events in Nuremberg dominated the front pages. *Der Montag* expressed the view that the rally was Germany's true Reichstag. Alfred Hugenberg's *Lokalanzeiger* claimed that the rally had put the outside world under its spell. According to the *Börsenzeitung*, the congress had demonstrated "the magic spell of the master race." *Der Angriff*, Goebbels' propaganda newspaper, stated that the Nazi party was facing the world not only as a party, but as a Reich represented by a party. The story of the rally was reported in all the leading European newspapers. A great many of them carried Hitler's speeches in translation. Intermingled with skepticism in these reports was a tone of admiration for the organization and theatrics of the rally.

The New York Times' correspondent ended his series of articles by reflecting on the political significance and ramifications of the events he had just witnessed. He pointed out that it had been difficult to convey the spirit of Nuremberg and the new Germany in brief news dispatches to the American public, which lived in a world where two and two still made four. He was bewildered by this "brown world," which was trying hard to make the total something else, and was convinced it was succeeding. He tried to draw some conclusions from the many impressions of the past few days.

One inescapable conclusion from what could be seen here in the last few days is that the tide is at flood again. A few flimsy barriers, the strongest of which seems to be economic, are holding back the waters, but who can tell what unexpected turbulence may sweep them all away? All the talk here has been of peace, yet the whole atmosphere has been far from peace-loving or peace-making. Germany may still be economically weak, but she is again spiritually strong and wholly united in her strength. . . . A second inescapable and quite positive conclusion is that National Socialism as the supreme power in Germany is there to remain for a very long time. . . . Anyone who dreams of an increasingly difficult economic situation forcing Hitlerism out in the coming hard winter should awaken quickly, for the reality no longer matches the dream. It will be a hard winter here, and for the wealthy as well as the poor. Indeed, it may be hardest for those once wealthy, should the needs of the men who fill the Nazi ranks become greater. But the power, including the power of distribution, will remain where it now is. . . .

Which leads to a third conclusion, tending with reluctance toward prophecy: there will be no moderation of Nazi policy in the direction of greater liberality. The Nazis have as definitely done with liberality as with liberalism. They find its reverse serves them better.[19]

Starting in 1933, the Nuremberg rallies were to rise to extreme importance in the life of the nation; they were to develop slowly into a national institution. The ideological discussions at the 1933 rally remained insignificant. The speeches were, for the most part, dull; they rehashed old themes and hate slogans of the party. The main emphasis of the 1933 rally lay in the celebration of the Nazi victory over democracy. It was a splendid display of newly gained power and national solidarity.

8   THE PARTY DAY OF UNITY
1934

The National Socialists gave two titles to the party congress of 1934: the Party Day of Unity and the Party Day of Power. The period between September, 1933, and September, 1934, had seen Hitler's concentration of power and the attempt to mediate between conflicting forces in the party.

At that time, the most serious tension existed between the SA and the army. When the National Socialists seized power, Hitler's Storm Troopers and other radical groups felt that they were not adequately rewarded for their part in achieving victory. They resented the fact that many recent converts to the party were given key positions in the new state, while they were left outside. The veteran SA leaders had come up from the ranks of the Freikorps, and they despised the army officers' clique, who were members of the aristocracy. The leaders of the army, on the other hand, regarded the SA as an association of hoodlums and street brawlers.

Although Hitler felt indebted to the SA for having stood by him in the years of crisis, he was dependent on the army to keep him in power. He had not forgotten how dangerous it could be to have the army against him, since it had been instrumental in crushing his attempted *Putsch* in 1923. He foresaw that in the event of Chancellor von Hindenburg's death, he would need the backing of the military chiefs to attain supreme power in Germany.

On April 11, 1934, Hitler accepted an invitation to watch naval maneuvers from the cruiser *Deutschland*. General von Blomberg, the Minister of Defense, General Freiherr von Fritsch, and Admiral Raeder, the commander in chief of the navy, were also on board. It was on this occasion that Hitler came to terms with the German generals—being promised his succession to the chancellorship in return for suppressing the plans of Roehm, who wanted to subordinate the army to the SA. The army's position as the sole center of armed power in the state would be assured.

In the early part of June, Hitler ordered the SA to go on leave for the month of July and to return to their duties in August. Roehm announced that he intended to go on sick leave. During their vacation, the SA were not allowed to wear uniforms or to participate in any demonstrations. It is difficult to make a clear appraisal of the events that led to the thirtieth of June, when the SA and many of Hitler's opponents were removed from their position of power, for the preparations for the purge were cloaked in deepest secrecy.

During the last days of June, the carefully prepared action began: Roehm and his followers were assassinated on the night of June 30, and hundreds of executions and arrests followed throughout the country. Among the victims were Gregor Strasser and General von Schleicher. Viktor Lutze succeeded Roehm as chief of staff of the SA; under his leadership, the SA played an insignificant role. When Hindenburg died, on August 2, Hitler's goal was reached: the office of president was merged with that of chancellor, and it was his. On August 19, when the German people were asked to approve by plebiscite Hitler's assumption of Hindenburg's office, an alleged 89.93 per cent cast their vote in favor. About 4,250,000 had the courage to voice their disapproval. Another 870,000 spoiled their ballots.

The 1934 rally, which was the first to run a full week, had been planned since April by a committee under Rudolf Schmeer.[1] On

September 4, the eve of the first day of the rally, the party gave a reception in the Karthäuser Church for the foreign press; reporters from all the major newspapers of the world were represented.[2] Ernst Hanfstaengl, Hitler's foreign-press liaison officer, welcomed the journalists. He, an official of a state-controlled press, lectured the foreign correspondents on the true functions of journalism. He then praised, in the language of a travel agent, the beauties of the town of Nuremberg. *The New York Times'* correspondent wrote: "[The speech] revealed Dr. Hanfstaengl at his best and he lapsed into a fervent rhapsody as he acclaimed the charms of Nuremberg and dismissed his foreign visitors with the admonition to draw inspiration from the 'the moss-covered moats and dreamy portals and babbling fountains' of Nuremberg."[3]

Otto Dietrich, the party's official press chief, spoke next. He scathingly attacked discrimination against National Socialist Germany in the foreign press. He emphasized that he did not deny the right to objective criticism, but he resented overt distortion of the truth. He asked for recognition abroad of the party's social achievements in Germany. He proudly pointed out that strikes and lock-outs had become unnecessary since the party had taken over. In its first nineteen months in power, National Socialism had given jobs to 4.5 million workers, and the number of unemployed had sunk below 2.5 million. The total value of the building materials produced in Germany between 1933 and 1934 increased by 50 per cent over the previous year. With the help of the Strength through Joy program, 1.5 million Germans had been able to vacation abroad between April and August. The buying power of farmers had increased 20 per cent since the National Socialists had come to power. In July, 1933, Berlin had reported 7,096 robberies; this figure had declined by July, 1934, to 3,000. Marriages had increased by 24 per cent during 1934.[4] It is as difficult now as it was then to separate propaganda from truth in these statements.

The party's publishing firm, Eher Verlag, had arranged an extensive exhibition of propaganda material in the Museum of Transportation for the benefit of the visitors. It displayed all printed matter relating to the party—books, photographs, propaganda leaflets and pamphlets, as well as pictures and manuscripts of Dietrich Eckart, one of the earliest party members, who died in 1923.

One whole showroom was dedicated to Hitler's *Mein Kampf.* Visitors saw all the steps in the book's publication: the handwritten manuscript, the corrections of the publisher, the sketches for the jacket, and, finally, the finished book.

A pamphlet written in 1519 by Martin Luther, *Jews and Their Lies,* was exhibited in a glass case.[5] To further emphasize their link with German tradition, the National Socialists had brought to Nuremberg copies of the imperial insignia of Charlemagne which had been made by order of Emperor Wilhelm II. They were excellent replicas of the original imperial orb, scepter, and crown, and could be distinguished from the originals only by secret markings.[6] Hitler's reason for bringing these medieval symbols of imperial authority to Nuremberg was to demonstrate the historical bond between the First Empire of the ninth century and what he called the Third Empire, *"Das Dritte Reich."**

The organization committee was expecting 500,000 people to attend the rally—180,000 political leaders, 88,000 Storm Troopers, 12,000 SS men, 60,000 Hitler Youths, 50,000 Labor Service men, 120,000 party members, and 9,000 SS functionaries and special police to handle the traffic.

The prestige of the new regime abroad was demonstrated by the fact that more countries sent diplomatic observers to this rally than ever before. Japan, Turkey, Venezuela, Guatemala, Panama, Nicaragua, Luxemburg, Uruguay, Afghanistan, and Poland were among the newcomers.[7] In addition, 3,000 Germans attended who were living in foreign countries—in China, Japan, South Africa, and countries in North and South America. There was a special meeting on Saturday for these German party members from abroad. They were addressed by Rudolf Hess, and their eighty flags were consecrated by the NSDAP. The homage to Germans abroad became a regular feature of the rallies. The party wanted to have the closest possible ties with party members in foreign countries, who were to act as ambassadors for German ideology.

For the first time in party history, the High Command of the armed services attended a party rally as guests of honor. Among those attending were General von Blomberg, the Minister of Defense; General Freiherr von Fritsch, the Chief of Staff; Admiral

---

* During the early years of the movement, Hitler displayed great interest in the monarchy. Although the great majority of the German royal families regarded Hitler with disdain, the Emperor's son Wilhelm joined the party at an early date.

Raeder, Chief of the Admiralty; and commanders of all army and navy divisions. A detail of ninety-six officers had been assigned to service at this congress.[8]

This year's congress began with Hitler's arrival by plane from his summer home in Berchtesgaden late in the afternoon of September 4. The welcoming ceremony was held in the large reception room of the Nuremberg Town Hall. This chamber had been the setting for many state ceremonies throughout the centuries and was considered a shrine of German history. Hitler's arrival was heralded, in medieval fashion, by the ringing of church bells and a bugle fanfare. In a brief speech to the welcoming committee, Hitler praised the beauties of Nuremberg and even made a poetic reference to the sparkling eyes of the city's men and women, its "dearest treasure." He expressed the hope that the congress would spread Nuremberg's fame still further. Visitors had the impression that this year, the black SS uniforms outnumbered the brown uniforms of the SA.[9]

The activities of September 5 began with the official opening of the congress. The first speaker was Rudolf Hess. His speech began with a hypocritical homage to Hindenburg.

I am opening the sixth congress of the NSDAP in respectful memory of the late President von Hindenburg. He was a great patriot and a leading general under Hitler when the party was organized. We National Socialists thank the old gentleman for his support. He will always live in our memory. We are thankful to the rest of the world for the sincere tributes paid him. Von Hindenburg was our foremost soldier. We remember him with the millions of men who gave their lives for Germany. Our actions are the fulfillment of their desires.[10]

Though one knows that Nazi propaganda speeches played havoc with the truth, it is nevertheless surprising to see how far they would bend it to their purposes. With Hindenburg dead only one month, and the memory of his true personality still quite vivid among hundreds of thousands of Germans, he was pictured almost as a senior SA man who had helped to bring about the revolution.

Then Adolf Wagner read Hitler's proclamation to the congress. It made an overworked distinction between "revolution" and "evolution." It said that no revolution can remain permanent without leading to complete anarchy. A revolution's only purpose is to destroy centers of power, whereas a genuine change of conditions can be brought about only by evolution. The proclamation did not define "evolution" precisely. It was used, like so many terms in totalitarian ideologies, as a vague catchword. The proclamation touched only lightly on the nation's economic problems. Instead, it offered a broad dissertation of the social achievements and cultural programs of the new regime. It praised the government's large road-construction and homestead programs, and the domestic production of raw materials to counteract the world boycott of the German economy. Yet the proclamation betrayed awareness of possible trouble when it concluded: "Whatever may happen, National Socialism does not intend to capitulate."[11]

Hitler's first official speech was given in the afternoon. Alfred Rosenberg presided over the meeting, which was dedicated to the cultural aspects of National Socialist policy. Rosenberg, in introducing Hitler, acclaimed the Chancellor as not only the greatest political force in Germany in the last 150 years, but also its most potent stimulus of art and culture.[12]

Hitler then spoke for more than an hour on the cultural goals of National Socialism. According to him, the function of National Socialism lay not in the political area alone, but also in the reshaping of the nation's cultural life. He rejected reliance on the forms and ideas of the past: the National Socialist state was thinking in the long terms of history and could afford to wait for its own creative impulse.[13] The only culture that had influenced the Nordic nations in a positive manner was that of the Greeks, who, he insinuated, were akin to the National Socialists. He claimed that re-education of the whole German nation would be necessary to condition it for its new cultural goals. And he added: "That which the National Socialist movement has accomplished will in fifteen years be regarded as the German miracle."[14]

He announced that the press in Germany had been placed entirely at the disposal of the new government, and he hailed this actual loss of freedom as an important step toward greater national unity and strength. It was in this context that he made the statement that was to become notorious for giving birth to the slogan the "Thousand-Year Reich": "The nervous nineteenth century has reached its end. There will not be another revolution in Germany in the next 1,000 years."[15]

He then warned churchmen who were opposed to the government's control of the church. He insisted that it would be illogical
to continue the system of separate provincial churches that had
been forced upon Luther under the multiple-state system; the
various provincial church groups should now be united into one
national church, the Reichskirche. From now on there was to be
only one state; the party demanded there also be only one church.
Thus, under the pretext of church unification, Hitler made a
blunt move for state control of the church. The ultimate goal,
which history did not allow enough time to materialize, was the
complete nazification of the church. A separate congregation called
the German Christians had been in existence for several years.
After the seizure of power, it received strong state support. Special
ministers were trained in National Socialist theological semi-
naries. Those Christians who did not conform were kept under
constantly increasing pressure, which soon grew into open persecution.

Lukewarm party sympathizers also came under sharp criticism:
"We will purify our National Socialist fraternity of all those who
give only lip service, of all those who are not absolutely devoted
to the National Socialist idea."[16] For the first time, the hitherto
hidden stranglehold of the totalitarian regime became visible. Before the seizure of power, the party had been grateful for any form
and degree of interest displayed toward its program; after the
purge, the party leaders demanded absolute obedience to the state.

Cultural policy was also a topic at the evening session of the congress. Hitler violently assailed Jewish intellectualism in his speech
at this meeting. He characterized the centuries since the Middle
Ages as a period of anarchy. He blamed Jewish intellectualism,
which had penetrated Europe during this era, for the inconsistent
attitude of European nations toward cultural problems. He stated
that the spiritual confusion began in the Middle Ages, when classical art was plundered and mechanically copied, which prevented
the development of autonomous art. "A pure race alone can develop high art,"[17] Hitler claimed, and then credited himself with
being the guardian and custodian of German art. Art now would
be controlled by the creators of the Third Reich—a threat that was
to materialize all too soon.

Toward the end of his speech, the Chancellor displayed his
ruthlessness even more openly in referring to the more than 4 mil-

lion voters who had cast their ballots against his assumption of presidential powers. He threatened annihilation of any opposition to the party. He ended his speech by claiming that Germany wanted peace and cooperation among nations, and he blamed small interest groups of profiteers for instigating wars.

Considering that a whole day of the rally was devoted to formulating goals for the National Socialist cultural program, the accomplishments seem extremely meager. Amid the flamboyant pageantry of Nazi flags, party uniforms, celebrities, and cultural representatives from all over the world, one would have expected the disclosure of far-reaching new programs. Instead, the familiar lower-middle-class ideas on culture, the well-worn tepid prejudices and narrow-minded views, were once again on exhibit. There was the usual denunciation of the German classical tradition, criticism of the Jews for retarding the development of an autonomous national culture, and the vague promise of a new creative impulse as the result of the purification of the race. It is evident that the old phrases, threats, and uncertain promises were intended to camouflage the absence of a serious cultural program.

On the following morning, delegates of the Labor Service assembled on the Zeppelinwiese for a special review. This was the first time that this organization participated in a party congress. The Labor Service had been founded in 1933; only one year later, it had 250,000 members, graduates of the Hitler Youth. From the more than 1,000 labor camps scattered throughout Germany, 52,000 representatives had been selected to attend the rally.

In his address to these young men, Hitler praised the achievements and goals of the new organization; he forecast a day when participation in the Labor Service would be compulsory for all men and women. Hitler stated that the most important function of the Labor Service was to help create a genuine community of all Germans. By bringing together young people from all classes, backgrounds, and provinces to work side by side on national projects, he hoped to awaken in them a sense of solidarity. This experience should also educate the individual to subordinate his selfish interests to a great national cause.

At noon, the spade-carrying columns moved into Nuremberg to march. For two and a half hours, Hitler and other party notables reviewed the march. *The New York Times'* correspondent wrote that this parade was by far the most striking exhibition of show marching during the entire rally. The men looked tanned and physically fit from their outdoor labor, and because of their youth and discipline they were even more impressive than the Storm Troopers.[18]

In his *Berlin Diary,* William L. Shirer gave a vivid account of the visual effects of this review. He described the reflection of the morning sun on the 50,000 polished spades, the long columns of bare-chested men standing perfectly at attention, then breaking into chants of ideological slogans and exhibiting extraordinary skill in goose-stepping—all to the spontaneous cheers of the spectators.[19]

Later in the afternoon, a group of party leaders addressed a meeting in the Luitpold Hall. Dr. Robert Ley, the leader of the Labor Front (the government organization that had replaced the trade unions), sharply attacked the policies and practices of the old trade unions. He charged them with bribery, embezzlement, and theft. He was followed by Goebbels, who made a lengthy speech on propaganda techniques, repeating the familiar ideas and principles he had presented many times before.

Dr. Gerhard Wagner then spoke on "race and national health." He pointed to three dangers that might bring about the downfall of the nation: a low birth rate, survival of the unfit, and promiscuity between the races. He deplored the fact that until now the government had inhibited the growth of the population, in the reactionary belief that this would benefit the economy. He maintained that only a nation strong in manpower can be strong in other ways. He quoted statistics according to which the low birth rate in Germany was connected with a high rate of unemployment. A populous nation, he said, offers a larger market to the economy. Dr. Wagner then passed on to his second and most delicate theme, the survival of the fittest—an idea that was to play an ever increasing role in Nazi ideology. He declared that millions of marks were spent annually for children and adults afflicted with congenital diseases, such as blindness, deafness, dumbness, and mental illness. In order to eliminate this financial liability to the state, he proposed a program to reduce, if not abolish, hereditary diseases in the future. Dr. Wagner did not divulge what plans, if any, the state had made to deal with its "unfit" citizens, but its practices in the following years showed that the party was never short of "solutions."

On September 7, some 100,000 new party functionaries and 30,000 members of the Hitler Youth arrived in the city, and the congress gained fresh impetus. In the morning, the congress took up a variety of topics. Dr. Bartels, of the public health service, lectured on health, race, and the philosophy of life. He pointed out that the state had the duty to protect its citizens against epidemics and other dangers to health, and that unfortunately epidemics did not discriminate between desirable and undesirable citizens; thus it was necessary to protect Jews as well as Aryans.[20]

The party's plans for extensive highway construction were also on the agenda. Dr. Fritz Todt, the Inspector General for Roads, reported that during the past year fifty-one highway-construction projects had been undertaken throughout the nation. He stated that 52,000 men had found employment so far in these projects, and another 100,000 were given work in the manufacture of necessary materials. He promised work for as many as 250,000 men on future projects.

Walther Darré, the Minister of Agriculture, declared that the nation's food supplies were sufficient to last through any war or boycott. He assured the assembly of continued economic growth in the future.

The climax of the rally was the meeting of the party district leaders that evening on the Zeppelinwiese. About 180,000 party members and some 250,000 spectators awaited Hitler's speech at 6:30 P.M. The party members came to attention when 21,000 party standards were carried through their midst toward the floodlit grandstand. The standard bearers represented the local party leadership, which totaled 700,000 functionaries throughout the nation. It had been expected that Hitler would make a major policy pronouncement at this session. Instead, he once again pledged cooperation with peace-loving nations and spoke of freedom and equality for the German people. He announced that the German nation had a God-given mission. He listed the virtues required for the party leaders as loyalty, obedience, discipline, a spirit of sacrifice, comradeship, and modesty.[21]

This evening marked the beginning of a new tradition of carefully staged visual propaganda. The Chancellor's speech was timed so that his closing remarks coincided with the arrival of darkness, and during the last words of his address, bonfires were lit along the horizon, and innumerable searchlights sent their broad beams into the sky, creating the illusion that the entire field was surrounded by a vast forest of luminous columns.[22]

The regime felt that in order to get firm control of the whole personality of the individual, a ritual had to be established that would reach the spectators' emotions. Since the ultimate aim was to replace religious emotions with ideological ones, ritual was of the utmost importance. In future rallies, increased effort was made to provide climactic moments that would blend the figure of Hitler, his words, and the sound of his voice with startling visual illusions, in order to mesmerize the masses into an almost religious frenzy of patriotism.

After 200,000 men had taken their oath of allegiance to Hitler,[23] the Chancellor was driven slowly back into the city. The route was lined with spectators who had been waiting for hours to see him. The men in the stadium lit their torches and followed the Chancellor's car in a ten-mile-long procession into Nuremberg.[24] The torch bearers marched twelve abreast, and this gigantic column of political leaders was joined en route by an estimated 500,000 spectators. A writer in the *Völkischer Beobachter* rendered his impression of the unusual sight: "The torch parade, seen from a hill above the city, looked like a river of molten, bubbling lava which slowly finds its way through the valleys of the city."[25]

On the following morning, Hitler addressed 2,000 women politicians at a meeting in the Congress Hall. He again blamed the Jews for having encouraged women's participation in politics. Whereas the liberals, he said, reserved a great number of functions for women in the state, the National Socialists saw but one, the bearing of children. While men make their supreme sacrifice on the battlefield, women make their highest contribution to the nation when they give life to a child. He concluded that democratic liberalism endangered the moral integrity of women by implicating them in parliamentary conflicts.[26]

The afternoon ceremonies were devoted to the youth rally. *The New York Times'* correspondent reported that of all the convention events, the youth rally was easily the most enthusiastic.[27] Since early morning, the various contingents of the Hitler Youth had begun to fill the Stadium. The delegations from the Saar had been strategically placed opposite the speaker's platform, and were seated in such a way that the letters on the girls' blouses spelled out the word "Saar."[28] A decidedly military atmosphere was noticeable at the youth meeting. In addition to wearing their usual uniforms, the youngsters carried knapsacks, and each group was accompanied by a boys' military band. The youth formations had to stand and wait for Hitler's arrival from 8:00 A.M. until 11:00 A.M. Quite a few of the young delegates fainted during this waiting period because of the heat and the physical strain. [29]

Baldur von Schirach, the head of the Hitler Youth movement, opened the meeting by greeting the Chancellor. He then praised the delegates for their achievements in the past and commended them for having attained one of their more important goals: discipline. He declared the overcoming of social barriers to be one of the movement's main objectives. He finished his address by citing Hitler as the model upon whom the youth of Germany were to mold their lives.[30]

Then Hitler gave a speech outlining the kind of life he wished the German youth to strive for:

> We want to be a peace-loving people, but at the same time courageous. That is why you must be peaceful and courageous at the same time. We want our people to be honor-loving; to that end you must, from earliest childhood, learn the conception of honor. We want to be a proud people, and you must be proud; proud to be the youthful members of the greatest nation. We want an obedient people, and you must learn to practice obedience. We want a people that is not soft, but hard as flint, and we want you from early youth to learn to overcome hardships and privations. There must be no classes or class distinctions among our people, and you must never let the idea of class distinctions take root among you. All we expect of the Germany of the future, we expect of you. We shall pass on, but Germany will live in you.[31]

The speech, delivered in Hitler's peculiar style of jabbing, short sentences, was frequently interrupted by cheers. At the end of the meeting, Hitler passed through the ranks of delegates and shook hands. He was then driven once around the Stadium, so that everyone could see him.[32]

Sunday, September 9, was the Day of the Storm Troopers; it was the climax of the rally. This year's SA rally was a particularly sensitive affair, since the recent Roehm purge had left its shadow on the organization. The delegates, 97,000 SA and 11,000 SS, began to fill the Luitpold Arena at 7:00 A.M. The first part of the ceremony was dedicated to laying the wreath in honor of the heroes of World War I and those who had lost their lives in the struggle for power. Once again, the party's skillful use of pomp and ceremony was shown, as to the roll of muffled drums the standards were paraded down the middle aisle to the War Memorial. As the assembly stood at attention, Hitler, flanked by Lutze and Himmler, walked slowly down the center aisle to place the wreath at the foot of the monument. After a few moments of silence, the three men turned around and marched back toward the assembly, while the banners were raised and the bands played the "Badenweiler Marsch"—Hitler's favorite march, which was played at all his entrances and exits on the party stage.[33]

In his address, Hitler set out to disperse rumors that he planned to disband the Storm Troopers. "Only a madman or a conscious liar can say that I have any such intention or that anyone ever had any intention of destroying the organization that we ourselves have created in long years of effort."[34] He told his listeners that the party was now so firmly entrenched in Germany that no power could conceivably overthrow it. He referred to the delicate matter of the purge. A shadow, he told his audience, had threatened the unity of their organization, giving the party's enemies the impression that the movement was faltering.

> First, the Storm Troops have had no more to do with this threat to the party than any other institution. Secondly, I want to show that my relation to you is the same as during the last fourteen years, comrades. Thirdly, I hope to demonstrate to our enemies that the National Socialists stand firm together. . . . All those who think that rifts have appeared in our unified movement are badly mistaken. Nothing in Germany can break our strength; when anyone betrays the spirit and purpose of our movement, when he betrays the spirit of my Storm Troops, that will be reckoned to the account not of the Storm Troopers but of the individual who dares to betray them.[35]

It must have been clear to his listeners that his veiled allusions to a betrayer of the "spirit and purpose of the movement" were directed against Roehm.*

---

* William L. Shirer gives an interesting eyewitness account of the tension between the party leadership and the SA on this morning. "Hitler faced his stormtroopers today for the first time since the bloody purge. In a harangue to 50,000 of them, he absolved them from the Roehm revolt. There was considerable tension in the stadium and I noticed Hitler's own SS bodyguards were drawn up in force in front

After the speech, Hitler proceeded with the now familiar ritual of consecrating the party flags and standards.[36] Then Viktor Lutze, Roehm's successor as head of the SA, made a brief speech in which he recalled the rallies of the past and pledged loyalty to Hitler in the future.[37] Shirer reports that when Lutze addressed the men in his shrill and unpleasant voice, he got a cool and indifferent reception.[38]

After the ceremonies in the Luitpold Arena, the SA prepared for a three-mile parade into the city. The streets were, as usual, lined with a great number of spectators. Shortly before 11:00 A.M., Hitler arrived, standing up in his car and saluting the people. He was followed by a motorcade of party officials, representatives of the army and navy, and visiting diplomats. The march past of the men lasted more than five hours. In the afternoon of the same day, a meeting in honor of the war veterans was held in the Congress Hall. Upon entering the hall, Hitler made his way at once to the section where a group of men who had been blinded in the war stood at attention, and shook hands with them.[39]

In the evening, the newly formed Strength through Joy group provided entertainment for the crowds. Four groups of 200 people each, of all ages and both sexes, demonstrated gymnastic exercises on the big stage of the Congress Hall. Many in the audience climbed on the stage and joined in the show.

A more serious act was put on by several choruses that chanted the history of the National Socialist revolution. Costumed groups acted out the scenes and showed in tableaux the Germany of yesterday, today, and tomorrow. During the finale, torches were lit and a bonfire built. Choirs entertained the audience with German folksongs and party songs. At the end of the day, there was one of the biggest fireworks displays ever seen in Germany.

The last day of the rally was dedicated to the army; with its inclusion this year, the pageantry of the rallies took on its final form, from which it did not deviate throughout the 1930's. Several hundred thousand spectators gathered in the Zeppelinwiese, where the army was to demonstrate its weapons and capabilities. The maneuvers began at 10:00 A.M. At the opening of the exercise, a detachment of cavalry charged onto the field to the blaring of

---

of him, separating him from the mass of brownshirts. We wondered if just one of those 50,000 brownshirts would not pull a revolver, but not one did." (*Berlin Diary*, p. 18.)

martial music. In order to demonstrate techniques of modern warfare, machine guns and mine throwers were exhibited. Members of a communications battalion explained the functions of these weapons. Then the artillery displayed its skill in target shooting; this was followed by a motorcycle group showing field routine. As a grand finale, all the different branches of the army were combined for mass maneuvers. Hitler was not present at the morning exercises, but the maneuvers were repeated in the afternoon for the Chancellor, General von Fritsch, and Hermann Goering. The foreign diplomats who were invited to the afternoon exhibition were duly impressed. At the conclusion of the maneuvers, the troops paraded their colors and bands.[40] As Hitler shaped the Reichswehr into his formidable Wehrmacht, the military displays at future rallies became increasingly impressive.

According to Shirer, it was difficult to exaggerate the frenzy of the 300,000 spectators as they watched their soldiers in action;[41] the enthusiasm was genuine, since it was the first time since the Versailles Treaty that Germans were able to see a large contingent of their army in exercises.

A serenade in Hitler's honor was the finale of the party congress, on the evening of this last day. At 10:00 P.M. eight bands arrived at the square in front of the hotel Deutscher Hof. The musicians carried torches. Hitler listened at his window as they played a medley of German marches and military songs. The concert concluded with the German taps, which dated from the seventeenth century. The elaborate interchange of the solo bugle and the band culminated in a somber drum roll and the chorale "Ich bete an die Macht der Liebe."[42] This torchlight serenade on the final evening became a tradition at future rallies.

Starting with the 1934 rally, the reactions of the foreign press were no longer made available to the German people. The party chose what favorable comments it could find and published them in the *Völkischer Beobachter*. To give the impression that the international press was on its side, the party rephrased or distorted articles without referring to any particular newspaper. The press reactions were merely published under subheadings of the countries in which they allegedly appeared. The *Beobachter* published vague, positive reactions to the 1934 rally from England, France Hungary, and Spain.[43]

The Nuremberg rallies reached their final form with the party congress of 1934. All the basic ingredients had been added; now, the party hoped, they would harden into a tradition. The Roehm purge had left awkward gaps among the participants that all the stepped-up pageantry was not able to distract attention from, and there was tension in the air. But Hitler seemed well in control of the situation.

The effects of this grandiose party congress were to be devastating. The irrational adulation and deification of Hitler demonstrated during this hysterical week increased Hitler's megalomania; he felt he could now whip the German masses into any frenzy, that they would carry out any order he might give them.

9 THE CELLULOID IMAGE

The masters of propaganda in Berlin recognized in film a formidable new means for mass persuasion. In the early 1930's the movies were fast gaining in popularity throughout the Western world and could easily be turned into a most effective propaganda medium.

A Reichsfilmkammer (Chamber of Films) was set up in Josef Goebbels' Ministry of Propaganda. It controlled every phase of film-making and distribution, including production, research and technical affairs, shorts and propaganda production, foreign distribution, and non-commercial exhibition. All persons involved in the industry were registered in the Filmgruppe, a National Socialist union for film workers. A Film Credit Bank was established for the financing of movies. In 1934, a national film law was passed, which enabled a censorship committee in the Propaganda Ministry to judge every film shown or produced in Germany. Six grades of commendation were introduced. A film could be labeled "particularly valuable politically and artistically," "valuable politically and artistically," "valuable politically," "valuable artistically," "valuable culturally," or, finally, "of educational value." To the party, the greatest value of a film was obviously its political content.[1]

Some of the earliest propaganda movies made under Goebbels' direction were *Storm Trooper Brandt, Hitler Youth Quex,* and *Hans Westmar.* One of the first ventures of this type was *Blutendes Deutschland (Bleeding Germany).* It was made shortly after the Nazi seizure of power and depicted the struggle of the NSDAP against the political forces of the Weimar Republic. The film reminded the Germans of the historical roots of the Franco-German conflict by showing scenes from the war of 1871, after which the victorious German generals compelled the French to sign a peace treaty in the Hall of Mirrors at Versailles. World War I was described as a war of revenge forced upon the Germans by the French. The senseless brutality of the war was presented in some impressive documentary footage of the fighting in France. By far the greatest part of the film dealt with what were allegedly the consequences of the Versailles Treaty. Large industrial cities in Germany were shown after production had been stopped, and the misery of the unemployed workers and their families was blamed on rich Jewish exploiters, whose luxury was contrasted with the poverty of the proletariat. Some highlights of the street fights against the Communists and the police were carefully selected to show the SA men in a heroic light. Scenes from Horst Wessel's funeral were skillfully used to arouse public resentment of the "death of a martyr." As an example of the growing strength of the party, a meeting of nationalist groups with Hitler in 1931, at Brunswick, was shown. The film ended with the victory parade held in Berlin on the evening of January 30, 1933, in honor of Hitler's accession to the chancellorship.

Very little documentary film is available on the party meetings of the 1920's. This was partly due to the fact that film-making was in the early stages of development and was still an expensive medium for an obscure political party. As far as is known, the first three Party Days were not filmed at all. There are only a few amateurish clips of the Party Days of 1927 and 1929. The 1929 rally was shown in less detail than the one in 1927, possibly because of the great amount of violence in 1929.*

It was not until 1933 that film became of great importance to the Nazis. There is no doubt that the painstaking organization of the rallies, the enormous effort to choreograph the masses in perfect clockwork motion against a background of expensive and spectacular scenery, was done not merely for the momentary effect on participants and visitors, but also to be recorded on film for domestic and international propaganda. Leni Riefenstahl, who was to produce the films of the rallies during the 1930's, wrote that "the preparations for the party conventions were made in connection with the preparations for the camera work."[2]

In the late 1920's Leni Riefenstahl was a budding young movie actress-director. She had achieved some fame by making a number of well-photographed movies about the Alps. Among her most popular titles were *Die weisse Hölle von Pitz Palu, SOS Eisberg,* and *Das blaue Licht.* According to her own statement, in an interview given to Budd Schulberg in 1946,[3] she first met Adolf Hitler in 1932. He asked her to his apartment in Berlin and expressed great admiration for her work. Hitler was such a movie fan, Riefenstahl intimated, that he was in the habit of seeing a movie a day until the beginning of the war. After complimenting her on her work, he tried to enlist her talents for the filming of party activities after he gained power. Riefenstahl recalled the exact words of his invitation: "Very soon now, in a year or two, I am going to be the leader of Germany. And when I am, I want you to make pictures just for me, just about me and the movement." Riefenstahl accepted, and within the next few years she moved into the position of top film executive of the party.

In 1933, she made the first full-length movie of a party congress. In an interview published in the *Völkischer Beobachter,*[4] she said that for the first time an attempt would be made to record the living reality of a party congress on film. She planned to go far beyond the reporting style of the regular newsreels. Instead of covering an event with random shots, she intended to base her movie on a carefully prepared script. She told the reporter about the great number of technical problems she and her crew had en-

---

* Participants at the rallies were not allowed to take motion pictures, although they could take photographs. Quite a number of amateur photographs of the rallies are still in existence.

countered in their work. It was very difficult to provide sufficient lighting for indoor shots without turning the meeting hall into a film studio. In order to do justice to the mass meetings in the Luitpold Arena, she had to distribute thirty cameramen on high scaffolds throughout the field. To obtain a maximum of useful film sequences, she had to calculate a shooting schedule for each individual camera. The monotony of the long parades and mass scenes was to be broken by shots of the beauties of Nuremberg, and by close-ups of the faces of individual participants. In an interview the following year,[5] she mentioned that she had found it impossible to film all the activities of the rally, and that it had been a painstaking project to select the most effective scenes.

Unfortunately, very little is known about this first film Riefenstahl made for Adolf Hitler. It is uncertain whether the film, called *Sieg des Glaubens (Victory of Faith)*, was ever exhibited publicly. The change in party leadership that occurred before the rushes were finished may account for the official withdrawal of the film: Ernst Roehm, the purged head of the Storm Troopers, must have played a feature role in the movie. It is even possible that the rushes were never printed, because to this day researchers have failed to turn up a single copy of the film.

Though the government suppressed the 1933 film, the following year Leni Riefenstahl made a film of the 1934 rally, called *Triumph des Willens (Triumph of the Will)*. This time she avoided the mistakes that had been made in the first film. She made more careful preparations, and the filming itself was less hastily done than that of *Sieg des Glaubens*. The party rehearsed the mass displays even more carefully than before. It seems safe to assume that the extraordinary show was planned and organized to create a powerful propaganda film that could, this time, be shown around the world.

An interesting source for the story of the filming of *Triumph of the Will* is Leni Riefenstahl's book *Hinter den Kulissen des Reichsparteitagfilms (Behind the Scenes of the Rally Film)*, published in Munich in 1935.[6] She writes that her staff consisted of sixteen cameramen, each with an assistant. Thirty cameras were used to film the events. Four complete sound-equipment trucks were at her disposal, and a huge number of spotlights. Twenty-two private cars were also assigned to her crew. Altogether, 120 people, including sixteen special news photographers, worked on the film. The book also provides insights into the preparations for the filming. Work on *Triumph of the Will* was begun in May, 1934. The crew arrived in Nuremberg one week in advance in order to mobilize all available fire equipment, the transit system, and the utility departments. They intended to film the approaching marching groups from all angles by using the long ladders on firetrucks or from moving streetcars. Julius Streicher put a house at the crew's disposal to be used as a film headquarters.

Since rally events could not be repeated, the cameramen had to do their best not to waste important scenes. They worked according to a carefully calculated schedule, but, in a way, each was his own director while he was filming. In order not to be conspicuous amid the uniformed masses, the cameramen wore SA uniforms. In her book, Riefenstahl listed the various devices she employed in achieving as great a variety of camera angles as possible. Her camera crew used the new techniques of wide-angle and telescopic lenses to catch the reactions on people's faces when they were unaware of being photographed. Special wooden platforms were constructed on the rally fields, as well as at vantage points throughout the city, for unobstructed views of the marching columns. An elevator was built on a flagpole behind the main platform in the Luitpold Arena, to provide shots from different heights. Cameras were placed on the ground to take close-ups of the marching boots. In order to get adequate shots of the maneuvers during the Army Day, cameramen lay on the ground to photograph in close-up the galloping hooves and speeding motor cars. Cameramen sat on chairs mounted on pushcars, and were wheeled beside marching columns or into the crowds for candid shots. The Labor Service laid wooden tracks on the field; cranes ran along these tracks from which the cameramen tried for close-ups of the marchers. A camera tower was built in downtown Nuremberg, from which the eyes of the men could be caught as they looked at Hitler.

The cameramen faced a very difficult problem when they attempted to film the procession of the Gauleiters at night. In order to light the stadium properly, they would have needed ten times as much electricity as the city could put at their disposal. Therefore, cameras could only be focused on scenes of primary importance: the speaker's platform, the long rows of flags, the eagles, etc. A lighting problem of a different nature arose when the crew began to film the torchlight parade, for to use klieg lights on the marching columns would have spoiled the effect of the torches. In order to provide sufficient light, the director had magnesium torches distributed to the bystanders. However, when the parade began, it was discovered that the smoke from the torches was blowing into the faces of the guests of honor. Since burning magnesium is virtually unextinguishable, nothing could be done to relieve the plight of the coughing diplomats and high army officers.

Triumph of the Will was undoubtedly the National Socialists' most detailed film of a parade. It is probably one of the most powerful and at the same time most repulsive films ever made. Riefenstahl made use of the melodramatic camera techniques of the 1920's silent movies, coupled with the dramatic effects of Wagnerian opera. A long "overture" is played before the film begins, with the screen remaining absolutely blank. Then an aerial view of the city of Nuremberg is seen. Endless marching columns of Storm Troopers appear, approaching Nuremberg for the rally. Hitler's plane is shown as it descends through the clouds to land at the airport. The symbolism at this point is so crude that it is impossible for a viewer to take these scenes seriously today. One of the few scenes that has not lost its power is the procession of the flags during the Gauleiter meeting. The great advance of flags moving from the rear of the vast stadium, through the ranks of the columns towards the speaker's tribune, must have been challenging for the cameramen. Another striking cinematic effect was the sight of the armored division charging across the field during the Reichswehr maneuvers. Although Riefenstahl comments that bad weather prevented the crew from shooting more film on Army Day,[7] the very cloudiness of the sky gives these military scenes a sinister effect that is most fitting.

Despite Riefenstahl's sometimes excellent camera work and effective editing, the endless parades and show marching make the whole film rather tedious. Therefore a condensed version, about one-third the length of the original, was usually shown. Despite its cinematic merits, the film offers a frightening view of the National Socialist leaders and ideology. It is hard to believe that the film is meant as propaganda, and not as a travesty of Nazi Germany. The film provides an interesting study of the many faces of Adolf Hitler; he is shown in the beginning as the benign "father of the land," smiling at children and at men and women in folk costume, but his features distort into an ugly mask as he rants and raves during his addresses to the masses in the Stadium, or in the Congress Hall.

In his book on the German film, *From Caligari to Hitler*, Siegfried Kracauer discusses Riefenstahl's work. He points out her use of obvious Germanic imagery: " 'Triumph of the Will' . . . proves that in shaping their mass-ornaments, the Nazi decorators drew inspiration from the Nibelungen. Siegfried's theatrical trumpeteers, showy steps and authoritarian human patterns reappear, extremely magnified, in the modern Nuremberg pageant."[8] Kracauer observes that although the film seems, on the surface, a composition of newsreel shots, it "represents a complete transformation of reality, its complete absorption into the artificial structure of the party convention."[9]

On March 29, 1935, *Triumph of the Will* had its premiere in Berlin. Among the guests of honor were foreign diplomats, army generals, and high party officials. The band of Hitler's SS Honor Guard opened the show on the festively decorated stage.[10] This evening was to be the beginning of the film's conquest of a worldwide audience, but in fact only a small number of nations friendly to Germany ever showed it publicly. It was never exhibited in the United States, either before or after the war. However, since *Triumph of the Will* is the most elaborate film on the party congresses, documentaries on this period frequently show excerpts from its parade scenes to illustrate the character of the Nuremberg rallies.*

In the years after 1935, the party congresses took up the major portion of the weekly newsreels, since additional full-length films would only have duplicated the achievements of *Triumph of the Will*. The newsreels concentrated on highlights of the individual congresses, such as the reading of the anti-Semitic laws in 1935,

---

* During the war, Movie-Tone Newsreels made a film parody of Hitler and his Brown Shirts called *Germany Calling the Lambeth Walk*. Film clips from the 1934 rally and later parades were selected, and the movements of the marchers were synchronized with a popular dance tune, "Doing the Lambeth Walk." Changing the speed and direction of the film made long rows of somber SS men nimbly do a two-step, and columns of SA men do tricky dance steps forward and backward. Inventive Anglo-Saxon humor at work in a laboratory forced Hitler to withdraw his hand again and again when about to greet high party officials at a solemn state affair. Needless to say, the Nazis anxiously kept this film from German audiences.

the youth displays, the army maneuvers, and the ceremony for the dead. The 1937 rally, with its inauguration of the German Sport Stadium, parade of the German police, and attendance by foreign dignitaries, was shown in the greatest detail. Yet despite the tight government control over film production and distribution, and attempts to curb the import of foreign films, German movie-goers, like the majority of European audiences, preferred American films to the products of the Goebbels industry.

Looking at the immense amount of film material that survived the war, one is astonished to see to what degree the National Socialists recorded the events between 1933 and 1945. They filmed every phase of their rule in great detail. Previously, the camera had been used only sparingly to record historical events, and it had never been used for the purposes of political propaganda. With the untiring effort of the National Socialists to create their own image on celluloid, the documentary film became not only a medium of history, but a dangerous means of falsifying history.

10   THE PARTY DAY OF FREEDOM
1935

The period between the rally of 1934 and September, 1935, was marked by an uneasy lull. The party rank and file were still stunned by the recent bloody purge, and the German people faced a period of adjustment to the new regime. The atmosphere in Germany was generally one of uncertainty. Yet the government itself felt secure in its power at home, and it seemed that the time had come for it to reveal its hand in foreign policy.

Hitler refused to join the other European nations in signing an Eastern Locarno Pact, for he did not want to restrict his freedom of action. He skillfully played on Poland's fear of a German-Russian agreement, which might easily result in another division of her territory, and lured her into closer relations with Germany. Another decisive foreign policy step, in 1935, was the Nazis' demand for a plebiscite in the Saar territory, with the intention of annexing this region. In January, 1935, the people of the Saar voted themselves back into the Reich by a majority of 90 per cent, and the Saarland was formally occupied by the Germans on March 1, 1935. Hitler's next move came when the French government doubled the period of military service and reduced enlistment age; Hitler reacted eagerly, announcing the necessity of German rearmament under the pretext of national defense.

Hitler also tried his hand at diplomacy: a naval treaty was negotiated with England. The agreement stipulated that Germany could build up a fleet of ships equal to one-third, and a submarine fleet equal to 60 per cent, of that of the Royal Navy. Since the Treaty of Versailles had set much stricter limits on German naval strength and had prohibited altogether the construction of submarines, this agreement represented a significant victory for Hitler.

Hitler's major foreign policy move this year was demonstrated in his famous "peace speech" delivered on May 21 before the Reichstag. In this carefully formulated statement, he played on the European nations' gullibility and their hopes for peace. His speech was a willful and malicious deception in which he threw sand in the eyes of the great European powers with sensible suggestions and promises of peace. He pledged his cooperation in general disarmament and told how deeply Germany abhorred war.

Several months were necessary to prepare the parade grounds for the 1935 rally. On August 18, Hitler went to Nuremberg to inspect the construction work personally, and to meet with leaders of the rally's organization committee.[1]

The first arrivals at the 1935 rally were the Storm Troopers from Hanover, who reached Nuremberg on September 2.[2] A large crowd was on hand to meet them when their train pulled in. The streets were lined with spectators as, to the music of the band, the 230 men marched with their flags to their quarters. Much was made in the press over a seventy-year-old SA man who had walked 1,250 miles from his home town to attend the rally.[3]

In order to promote the cause of National Socialism among industrial labor, 10,000 workers from all over the country had been invited to attend the rally as guests of the party.[4] All their expenses, including transportation, were paid by the government. They attended the ceremonies of the Labor Service, the political leaders, the Storm Troopers, and the armed forces, as well as the folklore festival.

In order to make full use of the propaganda potential of the rally, the proceedings were covered live by radio.[5] The NSDAP selected those functions that were to be broadcast, and the announcers who were to describe them to a national radio audience. The first event to be covered was Hitler's arrival in Nuremberg. Roving reporters mingled with the spectators and made on-the-spot interviews.

About 4,000 party members from foreign countries attended the rally.[6] They went first to a three-day meeting in Erlangen, where they were familiarized with the recent political changes in Germany.

Another new feature of the 1935 rally was the national symphony orchestra,[7] which provided a musical background to the speeches and further emphasized the operatic aspect of the Nuremberg Party Days.

As in previous years, Hitler arrived in Nuremberg by plane. Since early afternoon on September 10, tens of thousands of people had been lining the streets hoping to get a glimpse of him. His plane circled over the city and then landed, shortly after 4:00 P.M. The band played the "Badenweiler Marsch," and the huge crowd cheered as Hitler stepped from the plane with Goebbels and Brueckner. Many of Hitler's associates were at the airport to meet him, including Hess, Dr. Ley, Himmler, Amann, Bormann, Streicher, and Wagner.[8] Observers were impressed by the ominous increase in SS bodyguards. Their number was estimated at 20,000. About 13,000 of them were detailed as honor guards along the routes Hitler followed. The SS also formed a cordon around Hitler's hotel to ensure his protection.[9] After his arrival, Hitler's first official function was the welcoming ceremony at the Nuremberg Town Hall. The chamber was festively illuminated by candlelight; as an orchestra played the overture to Handel's *Julius Caesar,* Hitler received a replica of the Imperial Sword—the original of which had for centuries been the pride of the city.[10]

In the evening, Hitler attended a gala performance at the Opera House. The party dignitaries arrived in dress uniforms, the women in evening gowns. The nation's leading opera singers had been summoned for this command performance of *Die Meistersinger.*[11]

At the formal opening of the party meeting in the Congress Hall the following morning, Adolf Wagner, as usual, read Hitler's proclamation.[12] The text indicated the lines the party was expected to follow in the near future. It spoke of the three enemies the Nazis had singled out during their fifteen-year struggle: Jewish Marxism and the parliamentary democracies akin to it, the politically and morally destructive Zentrum (the Roman Catholic Center Party), and certain elements of an incorrigible and stupidly reactionary bourgeoisie. The proclamation further stated that the party had hitherto treated its opponents too leniently; in the future, sterner measures would be taken to deal with them. (The first step toward the realization of this threat was to be taken during the session of this congress, with the passing of the anti-Semitic laws.) After the proclamation had been read, Hitler spoke. He pointed to the widening gap between church and state, and pledged to establish complete trade and economic independence for Germany in obtaining raw materials.

After the official opening of the congress, Rudolf Hess delivered the inaugural address. The speech was routine: it eulogized Hitler's achievements and Germany's new military prestige, and concluded with a vigorous attack on the Jews.[13]

In the afternoon, the cornerstone for the new Congress Hall was laid. The document that was placed in the stone said that the building would serve the party congresses for thousands of years to come.[14]

At a meeting in the evening, Hitler abandoned politics and military strategy and lectured his followers on art, especially on his pet theme, architecture.

> Art is not something that can be summoned and called off again at will. In a time of distress especially, art must be a spiritual support. The pyramids of Egypt and the proud structures of Babylon also were created when there was poverty. If you want to make a people proud, you must give it something to be proud of. History finds no nation really worth while except when it builds its own monuments.[15]

Hitler heaped scorn upon the Dadaists, Cubists, Futurists, and Expressionists, saying they were either fools or cheats, and that some were Jewish Bolshevists. Jews have never produced art, Hitler said; even their temples at Jerusalem were built by non-Jews.

The primary event of the second day was the Labor Service parade. It was the first organization to use the recently completed parade grounds at the Zeppelinwiese.[16] At 10:00 A.M., a fanfare announced Hitler's arrival. Konstantin Hierl, leader of the Labor Service, greeted Hitler and introduced the Chancellor to his associates. Then the march of the 50,000 Labor Service men began. (The men attending this year's rally were the first to serve under the new compulsory law for the Labor Service.) Each of the eleven divisions was headed by a band, which, as the columns approached Hitler, wheeled to the right and played the division past. The ceremony took nearly three hours. The labor battalions were dressed in gray-green uniforms with peaked Robin Hood caps; each man carried a spade on his shoulder.

When Hitler addressed the columns of Labor Service men, he referred to the 50,000 gleaming spades. He called the spade "a gun of peace" and "a weapon for domestic self-preservation." The spade, he said, was the instrument that most honors the nation, and he wished that all Germany could witness this spectacle.[17]

During the session of the congress late that afternoon, Alfred Rosenberg addressed the meeting, attacking Jews and Bolshevism.[18] The virulent anti-Semitic tone of his speech foreshadowed the drastic action Hitler was to take on the last day of the rally. The day ended with the annual torchlight parade by the political leaders. The huge procession began to form at 8:30 P.M., and Hitler reviewed the parade half an hour later, at a downtown square.

On the morning of September 13, delegates attended a congress session at which Goebbels spoke on the differences between National Socialism and Bolshevism. An editorial that had appeared in an English publication the previous month had listed the similarities between the two dictatorships—Communist and National Socialist. The Minister of Propaganda was infuriated by this comparison. In his speech, therefore, he presented his definitions of the two systems—and in such a way that he could attack the Western democracies and the Communists in one breath. Communism, in his opinion, tried to destroy a people's national and racial characteristics; it also considered personal property the main reason for the fluctuations in the world economy. Communists denied the value of the individual personality and postulated the cult of the masses. In contrast to this, the main concerns of National Socialism were personal property, personality, nationality, and race.

While Communism planned a revolution of all people and expressed internationally aggressive tendencies, National Socialism was concerned with Germany only, and was not interested in exporting either its ideas or its methods. Communism was strictly anti-religious, whereas National Socialism respected certain forms of religion. National Socialism, the Minister of Propaganda said, was a new form of European culture, but since Bolshevism was led by international Judaism, it was hostile to all cultural traditions. The most essential difference between the two systems was that whereas Communism promised the workers a paradise in the future, National Socialism had realized it in the present.[19]

The next speaker, Dr. Robert Ley, delivered a detailed report on the progress of the organization of the various labor forces in Germany.

At 5:00 P.M., 100,000 political leaders who had marched from their quarters with flags and bands assembled on the Zeppelinwiese to honor Hitler.[20] The ceremony was conducted with the usual pomp and attended by milling crowds. Dr. Ley introduced Hitler as the main speaker. In his brief address, Hitler expressed his appreciation for the loyalty the political leaders and their subordinates had shown him in the past.[21]

The most important event of the evening was the meeting of the party women in the Congress Hall. Hitler was introduced by Mrs. Gertrud Scholtz-Klink, the head of the National Socialist Women's Association. Hitler discussed the National Socialist theories on the role of women in the new Germany. He claimed that the Third Reich was breeding a generation of men who, because of their vigor and strength, would be more attractive to women. With the eloquence of a professional matchmaker he extolled the handsomeness and charms of his bare-chested Labor men. He then repeated the clichés that German women were the "eternal mothers of the nation" and "the eternal companions of men in work and battle." Catering to a certain conception of Teutonic heroism, he proclaimed with stale, romantic bathos: "We are willing to fight, but when we are wounded, you must nurse us." He concluded with his now familiar disqualification of women as parliamentarians and praised the task of bearing and tending babies as their highest triumph.[22]

On the following day, the feature event was the youth ceremony in the Youth Stadium at 10:00 A.M. Fifty thousand youngsters attended to hear Hitler's address. After this event, *The New York Times* reported: "A new German religion with God manifesting himself in an invincible German nation and with Adolf Hitler as his modern prophet appeared in the making tonight if Nazi party conventions and utterances could be taken as indications. The trend towards such a religious conception was marked in the developments of the day."[23]

After confessing his belief in a policy of nonaggression Hitler spoke about the powerful German student associations.[24] As *The New York Times'* coverage shows, his allusions were not understood by outsiders, but they must have been quite clear to the initiated. He was attacking these very influential student associations because, although they had been centers of rightist nationalism throughout the nineteenth century, they remained indifferent to the National Socialists in the early 1930's. "We do not evaluate a young man by the number of glasses of beer he can guzzle but by the punishment he can take, not by the number of nights he can spend cavorting, but by the number of miles he can march."[25] The pseudo-religious note that had struck *The New York Times'* correspondent was accented by the performance of a political oratorio, in which bands, speaking choruses, individual speakers, and singers were featured.

At 11:30 A.M., the German Labor Front held its third annual convention in the Congress Hall. Discussing wages and price problems, Hitler explained that as far as he was concerned, he would be only too happy if he could raise wages and permit producers to raise prices.[26] But, he said, the economic situation made such sudden improvements unlikely. In answer to the charge that he had destroyed the freedom of the individual, he said: "My critics say that I suppress freedom. No, I merely give real freedom by taking from a few their freedom to utter nonsense."[27]

A meeting was then called to celebrate the establishment of a Reichswirtschaftsrat (National Economic Council), which was composed of representatives of the Labor Front and the Reichswirtschaftskammer (National Economic Chamber). Hitler used a familiar political device to gain confidence and support—he flattered this politically important group. The German laborers were praised as the world's best; the fact that the workers' paradise had not yet materialized was due to the fact that only three years had elapsed since the regime came to power. Hitler added that it was better for human beings that not all their ideals be realized immediately.[28]

When the congress met at 3:00 P.M., Max Amann, who headed the Nazi press program, spoke on the relationship between state and press. He pointed out that the time was over when publishers could sell editorial and advertising space in their papers for a profit. Before the seizure of power, only 100 out of Germany's 3,000 newspapers had supported the party. He announced that from now on it was the duty of each paper to report closely every phase of the national movement that was sweeping through Germany. Amann concluded his speech by interpreting the National Socialist attitude toward freedom of the press. He stated that "freedom of the press in the sense of the Western democracies no longer exists in Germany." The elimination of this freedom was, Amann declared, not an accidental consequence of the National Socialist revolution, but an integral part of the party program. For the party, the press meant an essential propaganda medium, and its freedom consisted in the privilege of serving the nation.[29]

After Fritz Todt had reported on the increase of employment due to the construction of the Autobahn,[30] Hans Frank, the party's chief legal adviser and Commissioner of Justice, addressed the congress on changes in law and justice in Germany since the seizure of power.[31] He reported that the general trend had been away from the too liberal and "too humane" principles of the past, when the supreme rule was "no punishment without formal law." The new postulate was "no crime without punishment." Frank saw in the hardening of legal attitudes a beneficial influence on national morale. Decent citizens would not be affected by this greater strictness, and the lawbreaker would regard it as a deterrent.

Dr. Frank then informed his audience of two amendments to the penal code that opened the way to the type of Nazi legislation that was to turn Europe into a nightmare world. New laws demanding castration of sex criminals and sterilization of racially inferior people would be rigidly enforced, Dr. Frank announced. This was essential to safeguard the moral health of the nation.

The speech concluded with the usual invective against Jews, who were denied the right to practice law. Frank compared the

"ideal state of law and law enforcement" in Germany to the rigid
police state in Russia, where, he said, the rights of the individual
were denied by the government.

The rest of the day was dedicated to a folk festival. By 4:00
P.M., spectators had already moved in large groups into the Zeppelinwiese to secure seats. The activities resembled a giant three-
ring circus. Various party organizations exhibited their skills in
sports. In one section of the field, young men performed bicycle
exhibitions; exhibition games of soccer and handball were played;
girls of the Bund Deutscher Mädchen (Federation of German
Girls) performed calisthenics; other groups did show skating or
danced polkas in folk costumes.

The neighboring fields were turned into a midway, with sausage
stands, refreshment vendors, and beer tents. The fireworks in the
evening were, as usual, spectacular. This year's theme was the four
seasons. Blossoming bushes and flowers symbolized spring, large
fruits the summer, sheaves of grain the fall, and a large, fiery swastika the ancient Germanic heliotrope festivals in winter.[32]

The next day, Sunday, was dedicated to the SS and SA. The
day began with a parade of these two organizations at 8:00 A.M. in
the Luitpold Arena. Hitler and Lutze addressed the men and led
them in the ceremony honoring the dead. This part of the exercises ended with a march to a downtown square at noon.

At 6:00 P.M., the congress resumed its session. In the first address, Fritz Reinhardt praised Hitler for having reduced the stag-
gering number of unemployed, and commented on the new tax
laws and banking regulations. Otto Dietrich then elaborated on
the government's attitude toward the press, which was one of the
main issues at this rally. One speaker after another attacked the
right of the press to free expression. By deploring the press's tend-
ency toward sensationalism, and by lashing newspapers for having
criticized Hitler before he came to power, they snapped shut the
Nazi shackles on the press.

That night, the most significant meeting of the rally took place
in a stately room in the Kulturvereinshaus.[33] Hitler addressed the
members of the Reichstag, confronting them with perhaps the
harshest and most brazen legislation of this young fascist regime.
At the back of a raised stage adorned with an enormous swastika
flag, the presidential chair was taken by Hermann Goering. Members of the government and high-ranking party officials occupied

the front rows of seats. Hitler, standing before the microphones placed near the presidential chair, delivered a short, sharp speech on the Memel question and then proceeded to announce three laws.

The first was that the swastika was now the official emblem of the German state. The second imposed special conditions for full German citizenship that would exclude all Jews. The third prohibited the marriage of Aryans and Jews, as well as sexual relations between them, and forbade German women under forty-five to serve as maids in Jewish homes.

Because of their great importance, the last two laws—which were to become notorious as the Nuremberg Laws—are worth quoting here in full.[34]

The Citizenship Law

Congress has unanimously passed the following law, which shall be made public herewith:

1.1. Anyone is a citizen who is a subject of the sovereign German state, and in return owes allegiance to it.

1.2. Citizenship is acquired according to the regulations of the national citizenship laws.

2.1. A citizen is only that subject of the state, of German or related blood, who proves through his behavior that he is willing and able to loyally serve the German people.

2.2. Citizenship is acquired through the bestowal of citizenship papers.

2.3. Only a citizen is entitled to full political privileges according to the law.

3. The Minister of the Interior decrees, in concordance with the special deputy of the leader, the legislative and administrative regulations necessary for the enacting and amendment of the law.

Law for the Protection of German Blood and German Honor

Fully convinced of the fact that the purity of German blood is the premise for the future existence of the German nation, and pervaded by the uncompromising will to safeguard the German nation for the future, Congress has passed the following law, which shall be made public herewith:

1.1. Marriages between Jews and citizens of German or related blood are prohibited. Marriages in violation of this regulation are declared void, even if entered abroad in circumvention of this law.

1.2. Annulment procedures can only be entered by a prosecutor for the state.

2. Extra-marital relations between Jews and citizens of German or related blood are prohibited.

3. Jews are not allowed to hire female citizens of German or related blood under forty-five years of age as domestics.

4.1. Jews are prohibited from hoisting the national colors.

4.2. The showing of the Jewish colors is permissible for Jews. The execution of this privilege is guaranteed by the state.

5.1. Violations of Number 1 are punishable by jail.

5.2. Violations of Number 2 are punishable by jail.

5.3. Violations of Number 3 and Number 4 are punishable by prison terms up to one year and/or fines.

6. The Minister of the Interior decrees, in accordance with the special deputy of the leader, the legislative and administrative regulations necessary for the enacting and amending of the law.

7. The law will be in effect on the day after the public announcement, but Number 3 only on January 1, 1936.

Violent anti-Semitism had been part of the National Socialist doctrine from the very beginning of the movement, but with the proclamation of the Nuremberg Laws, which Hitler dictated to his congress and which were enthusiastically approved by his supporters, the party took its first decisive step against the Jews in Germany. This was to have far-reaching consequences. Only two years after having attained supreme power in Germany, the Nazis used the state's legislative machine to strip the Jews of their citizenship and thereby of their civil rights. With this gross abuse of the legal apparatus, the Jews were ousted from the protection and security of the society they had lived in, and were exposed to any form of prosecution and harassment the state might see fit to choose.

The 1935 party rally was climaxed with a display of the newly reorganized German army on Monday, September 16. It was clear that this brandishing of a growing army, equipped with the most modern gear, was carefully timed by the party leadership. "The army must preserve the power given to Germany and watch over it," Hitler told his followers in a speech that day. Great show maneuvers and parades were held in the Zeppelinwiese before thousands of spectators, invited guests, and members of the party organization. Altogether, 100,000 men and more than 100 war planes and heavy bombers participated in these exercises. The parade represented the thirteen services and included a small naval detachment from the officers' training school.[35]

The principal attraction was the first public display of some of the modern weapons with which the German armed forces were equipped, now that the limitations of the Treaty of Versailles had been repudiated. The display included a mechanized scouting detachment equipped with a new type of armored car, a detachment of mechanized artillery with fifteen-centimeter field guns and howitzers, a tank company, and an anti-tank gun detachment. Several of the mechanized units staged realistic engagements, which were carried out amid much noise to the delight of the crowd. A second war game, an air attack on a factory village, was interesting chiefly because it offered the first view at a Nuremberg rally of the new air force and anti-aircraft batteries.

At 6:30 P.M., Hitler addressed the closing session of the congress. In summing up the spirit of the rally, he pointed out that a modern army and a unified party were the bases of a strong Germany.[36]

As a special attraction, an exhibition of National Socialist publications had been shown to visitors throughout the rally. The great majority of the volumes dealt with World War I. To capture the public's attention, the technical process of printing the *Völkischer Beobachter* was shown. In another room, some of the leading Nazi magazines were on display—the *Illustrierter Beobachter, Die Brennessel, Der SA Mann, Das schwarze Korps,* and *Hitlerjugend.* Pen-and-ink drawings by Hitler were prominently shown. One room was dedicated to Hitler only. There was a bust of him, and his family tree was exhibited. A book on display told the history of Braunau, Hitler's home town, which had been bought by Germany from Austria in 1779.[37]

The *Völkischer Beobachter* carried a number of alleged foreign press reactions to the rally. Since by now the German press was completely controlled by the party, the public received only carefully screened foreign news items. The *Beobachter* reported that Paris was "impressed with the new Germany"; its discipline and the will to respect the ideals of the party were mentioned. Hitler's statement that the goal of the army was not to threaten the freedom of any nation but to ensure Germany's freedom had made headlines, the report went on, but the French press could not understand the reason for the new laws concerning the Jews.[38] The *Beobachter* told its readers that the Italian newspapers had been filled with reports of the rally, and that all speeches had been printed in translation, but that no comment on the new laws had yet been printed by the press in Belgrade, Vienna, Holland, England, or America. The London *Times* was quoted as saying that Hitler must be proud of the accomplishments of his party, especially of the rebuilding and new-found unity of the country. The *Beobachter* claimed that in Washington Hitler's speech was considered a declaration of freedom.[39]

All this shows again that the Nuremberg rallies were far more than annual party congresses surrounded by pageantry. The rallies were an exhibition of everything the National Socialist movement stood for—a carefully constructed showcase where party ideology and its effects on the masses could be displayed to the nation and to the world. The rally of 1935 is a good example. Before hundreds of thousands of loyal supporters, and before the eyes and ears of the world, Hitler proclaimed the drastic new legislation that was to initiate the methodical persecution of the Jews. By exhibiting a surprisingly modern and versatile army, Hitler convinced his own country and onlooking nations that he had the military force to back up his sinister principles.

This year's parades, displays, and speeches showed how far the National Socialist movement had come since 1923; Hitler's control over the party and the nation was incontestable. Alan Bullock wrote of this congress: "[Hitler's] speeches throughout the rally were marked by the confidence of a man sure of his hold over the people he led."[40]

1929

1933

1935

1939

1937

Party Day Medals

Party Member
Emmert-Nuernberg

Party Member
Schulze-Muenchen

SS-Sturmbannführer
Blumberg

SS-Standartenführer Lohse

Party Member Kropp

Party Member Gohdes

Hauptmann Dr. Treeck

Party Member Wollner

SA-Gruppenführer Juettner

Party Member Brauns

Party Member Schwarz

Party Member Seidel

Oberstfeldmeister
Dr. Seebauer

Reich Organization Leader
Dr. Ley

SS-Standartenführer
Rosener

Party Member Adam

Party Member Strang

Party Member Schmidt

Interior of the Congress Hall

Consecration of the flags at the first Party Day, Munich, 1923

SA at the 1923 rally

Hitler reviewing Storm Troopers at the 1926 Weimar rally

German Day, 1923

Hitler reviewing Storm Troopers at the 1926 Weimar rally

March past, 1927 rally

Consecration of the flags, 1929 rally

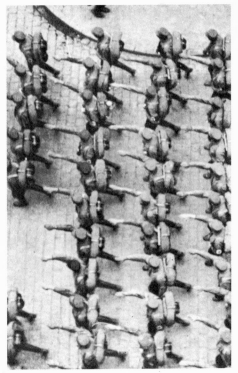

March past of the SA, 1933 rally

Street scene at the 1933 rally

Leni Riefenstahl, in 1934

Hitler and Leni Riefenstahl at a filming session in the Luitpold Arena, 1934

Model for the Army Field

Alfred Rosenberg

Viktor Lutze

Opening of the 1934 congress of delegates. Front row *(left to right):* Robert Ley,
Franz Schwarz, Heinrich Himmler, Viktor Lutze, Hitler, and Julius Streicher.
Second row: Wilhelm Bruckner, Hitler's bodyguard *(directly behind Hitler),*
and Martin Bormann *(behind Streicher).* At the speaker's stand: Rudolf Hess.

Section of one of the eagles being assembled for the 1934 rally

Army Day, 1934

Commemoration of the dead at the 1934 rally

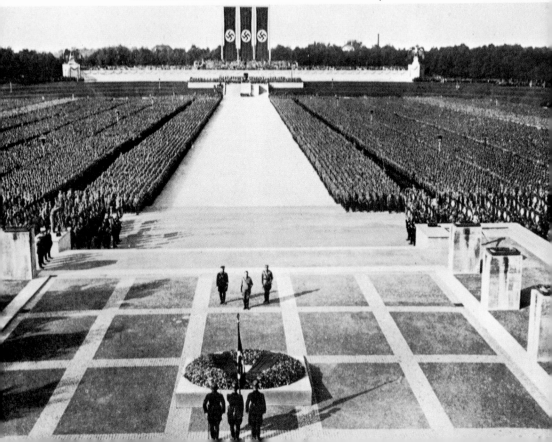

Hitler addressing a nighttime meeting, 1934

March past of the SA, 1934 rally

Hitler reviewing the torchlight parade at the 1934 rally; at the left, Rudolf Hess

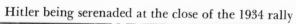

Hitler being serenaded at the close of the 1934 rally

Parade of the flags, 1935 rally

Army Day, 1935

Hitler Youth Day, 1935

The morning after the rally of 1935

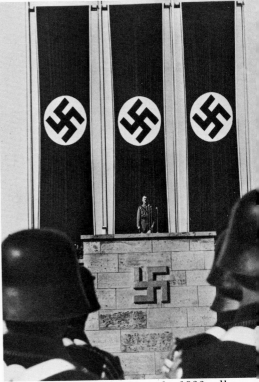

The "dome of light" on the Zeppelinwiese, 1936 rally

Hitler addressing the SS at the 1936 rally

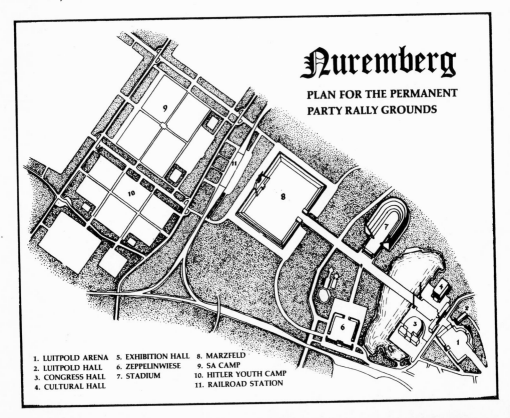

ꟓuremberg

**PLAN FOR THE PERMANENT
PARTY RALLY GROUNDS**

1. LUITPOLD ARENA
2. LUITPOLD HALL
3. CONGRESS HALL
4. CULTURAL HALL
5. EXHIBITION HALL
6. ZEPPELINWIESE
7. STADIUM
8. MARZFELD
9. SA CAMP
10. HITLER YOUTH CAMP
11. RAILROAD STATION

11   THE ORGANIZATION MANIA

Through a widespread network of bureaucratic cells, the totalitarian state establishes its hold over society. The more complicated and manifold the bureaucracy, the more effectively reduced are the functions of the individual official to a minute area of government—thereby guaranteeing that real power stays in the hands of the dictators.

The National Socialists understood the cohesive power of organization and became masters at its use. The National Socialist state had penetrated German society with a bureaucracy so highly organized that it had divided and subdivided the nation down to the smallest street block.

This ominous genius for organization found its most striking application in the preparations for and the conduct of the party rallies in Nuremberg. The rallies were planned by an organization committee headed by Dr. Ley. Each committee member had a clearly defined area of responsibility and was expected to plan his limited organizational detail to perfection. The offices of the organization committee were located at 1 Feldmarschall Hindenburg Platz. Dr. Ley's closest associate in this project was Heinrich Strang. Adam was responsible for financial planning. Kropp was in charge of ingoing and outgoing mail, allocation of parking spaces, and railroad transportation. It was his task to procure, in close collaboration with the railroad authorities, 480 special trains to carry participants from all over the country to Nuremberg; in addition, 220 special trains had to be set aside for the political leaders and members of the Strength through Joy organization. SA group leader Juettner was in charge of the preparation and execution of all parades during the rallies.

The vast canteen operations at the rallies were entrusted to Seidel and Franz Xavier Schwarz. Special contracts were given out to breweries and certain retail stores for the duration of the rally, and licenses were issued to 3,240 vendors. Besides providing food and refreshments, these two men organized the living accommodations. They had to place 240,000 men in nine camps and find lodging for them in 2,100 available tents.

The intricate job of planning city traffic during the hectic rally days was given to Rosener. He and his staff had to chart vast zones that were closed to public traffic; however, a large number of party VIP's had to be issued special permits to travel in these restricted areas. Rosener was also expected to create adequate parking space for the large number of vehicles that were brought into the city during these days. Ernst Schmidt was responsible for the contingents of foreign and domestic reporters who covered the events. Gohdes planned the annual parades of the 170,000 political leaders and the elaborate torchlight processions in the evenings. Wollner arranged the sessions of congress and the various special conventions for the one-week period. Brauns prepared living quarters in the city for the participants. All available hotels, private families, gymnasiums, and large public halls were used to accommodate the masses of visitors. Other members of the organization committee were Walther Schulze, in charge of propaganda, film, and radio; Lohse, in charge of SS parades; Blumberg, in charge of special services of the SS Engineer Corps, which constructed five large bridges for the rallies; Treeck, in charge of army maneuvers at the rally; Seebauer, in charge of the construction team of the Labor Service; and Emmert, in charge of the folk festivals.[1]

The much-admired discipline, show marching, and precise choreography of the vast masses at the rallies were by no means spontaneous manifestations of a national spirit. They were the result of long, grueling drills that were conducted the year round in the local chapters of the NSDAP. Participants were selected many months in advance. Men and boys were selected in towns and villages all over the country because they excelled in marching or as members of their local brass bands or music groups. Girls were selected because they were the best singers in their choirs or performed outstandingly in their athletic groups. Thus, from all the party's factions and activities, the outstanding members were chosen to represent their local organization at the rallies.

After the participants had been selected, they were endlessly drilled and rehearsed in their particular skill. They had to give much more of their time than was ordinarily expected of any National Socialist party member.* In the beginning, they would spend three evenings a week drilling, but as the rally drew nearer, this was increased to five nights a week; finally weekends were added, when musicians and singers would visit neighboring music groups to rehearse.[2]

The bulk of the rally participants were transported to Nuremberg by special trains; 500 were employed for the rally of 1938; they were backed up more than 100 kilometers outside the city.[3] Special groups were driven to Nuremberg by trucks. The departure and arrival procedures were minutely prepared, as can be seen from this eyewitness report.

During the last two weeks before the departure, every participant received several special slips with all necessary information about the trip, the arrival, and the quarters. There was a green slip on which were printed the province, the participant's unit (e.g., Hitler Youth Choir), his town, and his number—every participant was given a number. There was a yellow slip on which were printed the participant's name, home town, the number of the truck on which he would travel, his place of departure, time of departure, and the number of his seat on the truck. There was a red slip on which were his name, number, section of the tent camp in Nuremberg, number of the tent in which he was to sleep. There were, furthermore, all

* The compulsory time of service for the average member of any National Socialist group was two nights a week; for the Hitler Youth and Jungvolk, two afternoons a week.

kinds of coupons for meals, refreshments, special excursions, etc. The flat fee for myself for the trip, tent bed, meals, was twenty-five marks; anything else had to be paid for separately.

Our singing group was to gather for departure at 10:00 P.M. There were about fifty trucks waiting on a large square when I arrived. My group was assembled within ten minutes, and we boarded the truck within fifteen minutes, so that we were able to leave at around 10:30 P.M. The speed with which the actual departure was possible is remarkable, considering the great number of participants and trucks. However, the moment of departure was so well organized through the slips, numbered seats, etc., that the departure took place without the slightest delay. The trip itself was extremely strenuous, since the trucks had no springs, and the passengers sat close to each other on wooden benches.[4]

The arrival procedures and distribution of participants to their quarters is well described in a party publication of 1938:

On Saturday, the busiest of all days, seventy-one special trains arrived in Nuremberg in less than twelve hours. Each train carried about 800 men. Here precision and discipline were very important As soon as the trains came to a stop, the men were assembled on the platform with their packs on their backs, and the four-kilometer march to the camp ground was begun. After about an hour, the rows and rows of tents were visible. The men were glad finally to be at their destination. Many had been traveling more than twenty-four hours. Langwasser, the traditional camp ground of the SA, had been occupied by the Labor Service men during the early part of the week. After their departure, every tent had been cleaned and put in order again, and now it looked as if the camp had been built especially for the SA. Each county had made some decorations for their tent groups, many of them works of art which must have taken many hours of labor. The men were shown to their quarters. Since an exact plan showed the location of each group, this took only a very short time. Each man was given a "city directory" to enable him to find his way around; the "city of the 80,000" had fourteen streets, each named after a party member who had given his life for the party. All the entrances to this tent city were guarded, and only people carrying passes were admitted. Every SA man wanting to leave the camp ground had to show an authorized pass to the guards.[5]

The great difficulties in lodging and feeding these masses were described in an article that appeared in the *Völkischer Beobachter* in 1935.

To find eating facilities and sleeping quarters for the many thousands of party members was a colossal job. Metal bed frames and mattresses were bought for the mass quarters in factories and schools. They can be stored and used every year. Only a small percentage of the men were able to stay in private homes. The people of Nuremberg were asked to fill out a questionnaire stating any extra beds available. There are only a few hotels in the city of Nuremberg, and they have a combined total of only 2,000 beds; naturally, the hotels are reserved for the special guests.

How to feed many thousands of people at the same time poses the biggest problem. Each military or political group has its own field kitchen. The food was bought as far in advance as possible. One central committee did all the buying. . . . During the rally, all restaurants were to stay open around the clock, but no alcoholic beverages were to be served after midnight.[6]

To assure the smooth operation of the tent city, SA group leader Juettner issued a number of tent rules, by which each inhabitant of the city had to abide:[7]

1. All orders must be obeyed immediately.
2. The tents must be kept clean and tidy.
3. There will be no smoking in the tents at any time. Kerosene lamps, open fires, and cooking are not allowed in or around the tents. Swimming in rivers, walking through woods, driving faster than twenty-five km.p.h. in the camp grounds, are not allowed. Kitchens and washrooms of neighboring groups are not to be used. Daggers are not to be carried, but kept with the pack.
4. Fires must be reported at once. [A detailed description of the steps to be taken followed.]
5. Anyone feeling ill must report to the doctor at once. There are first-aid stations on every camp ground.
6. No one is allowed to leave the camp grounds without a pass. Upon return, everyone must report in.
7. Civilians are not permitted on the camp grounds.
8. Taps will be blown at 10:00 P.M. At 10:30 P.M., everyone must be in bed. Silence is requested. No visiting of neighboring groups is allowed after taps. Campfires must be extinguished.
9. In case of alarm, each group will assemble on the street outside the tents.

10. Breaks in water lines, disrepair of electrical outlets, etc., must be reported at once.

11. Each person will be asked to make a deposit for glasses and dishes in the canteen.

12. Lost and found articles must be reported at once.

During the rallies, the stores in Nuremberg were open from 5:00 A.M. until 11:00 P.M. There were strict regulations concerning street vendors.[8] All vendors had to have a license. Areas where vendors were allowed to set up their stands were carefully zoned by the police; in order to prevent main parade routes from being turned into bazaars, the number of permits issued was controlled according to available space. Vending within the limits of the tent camp was prohibited, and peddlers were forbidden to enter the grandstand of any rally ground while a meeting was in session. The police kept a close watch on the prices charged. Violators ran the risk of having their licenses revoked and their goods confiscated. During the folk festivals, all sales were prohibited.

Since souvenirs that could be carried from the Nuremberg rallies into the rest of the country were excellent propaganda, the party made a great variety of reasonably priced souvenirs and sold them at stands all over the city. The most popular were rubber stamps, postcards, book marks, and black-white-and-red pennants with swastikas for cars. No private vendor was allowed to sell articles connected with the NSDAP.

Strict rules of hygiene were enforced for all vendors who handled food. Beer, ginger ale, sparkling water, candies, and chocolate were available on the rally fields. Near the rally grounds, each province had built its own dining hall, where its local foods were prepared and served. The meal breaks were approximately an hour long; the cheapest and most popular dish was a bowl of pea soup.

First-aid services were well organized during the rally.[9] The Red Cross worked closely with the Hilfszug Bayern, a hospital group from Bavaria. A large number of first-aid tents were erected at convenient places. Nurses and medical assistants circulated through the crowds. Doctors were also on duty at strategic places throughout the rally grounds.

Sound amplification was one of the major problems at the outdoor meetings. The sound had to carry over many square miles and yet remain at even, pleasant volume. To accomplish this,

twenty loudspeaker systems were used. The high degree of fidelity
achieved was described by a visitor: "The power of the means
used for amplifying the sound was tremendous. For example, when
the master switch of the amplifiers was turned on in the quiet,
empty fields, the soft sound of a wristwatch ticking would make
the whole field resound as if it were the noise of boiler makers
hammering."[10] Large mushroom-shaped loudspeakers, constructed
to avoid echo effects, were designed for use in the large stadiums.

Every year, an impressive feat of teamwork was performed by
the Labor Service to prepare the Stadium for the army maneuvers
of the last day. After the last meeting, the Labor Service cleared
away the vast maze of loudspeaker cables, buried underground,
and took down hundreds of large public-address systems, so that
the army exercises could take place the following morning un-
hampered.

An interesting glimpse into the choreography of the gigantic
march past of hundreds of thousands of party members is furnished by a party document that details the whole procedure,
down to the posture of each individual man.[11] The document first
gives the order in which the formations of the various party groups
enter the parade. The required formations had to be formed on
the approach route to the main square, where Hitler reviewed the
parade. By the time the ranks moved into his sight, they were to
be twelve men deep, the distance between the marchers 114 cm
(thirty inches). (Diagrams of the distances to be kept between
individuals, between rows of men, and between the hundreds of
standard bearers are attached to the document.) The left hand of
the marcher was to be placed on the belt buckle; the thumb
was to be inside, behind the buckle, and the other fingers slightly
bent, with the finger-ends at the right edge of the buckle.

The document gives the exact timing of the cues for the hundreds of bands to begin to play—when they reached a certain distance from Hitler. The exact order in which the huge parade was
to disband, after each formation had passed Hitler, was also carefully prearranged.

All this effort involved great expense. In order to estimate the
over-all costs of an average rally, a German economist, Henry
Heuser, tabulated the following statistics for this study: he com-
puted his figures per unit of 80,000 people who attended the
rally:[12]

Travel expenses	$2,400,000
Food	160,000
Lodging	160,000
First-aid arrangements	10,000
Public utilities	20,000
Leaflets, papers, etc.	50,000
Total	$2,820,000

This figure may easily be rounded off to $3 million, since a large number of expenses, such as construction costs, are not included. The average attendance at a rally in the 1930's may be safely estimated at 500,000, which places the over-all cost, at a conservative estimate, at about $20 million.

This chapter merely touches the surface of the vast amount of organizational detail that went into the Nuremberg rallies. To analyze it thoroughly would require an entire book. For the purposes of this study, these few examples may suffice to give an idea of the calculation and planning behind the smooth functioning of these affairs.

12 THE PARTY DAY OF HONOR
AND FREEDOM
1936

The international scene was troubled by two major events during the period following the 1935 rally: Mussolini's invasion of Ethiopia and the Spanish Civil War. In October, 1935, Mussolini sent troops into Ethiopia to annex it to Italy's colonial empire, under the pretense of revenge for Ethiopia's attack on Italy in the 1890's. In July, 1936, a military group under Francisco Franco started a rebellion against the Spanish Republic that erupted into one of the bloodiest and most bitter civil wars in history. Immediately upon being informed of the rebellion in Spain, Hitler realized the great political advantage in helping to create a third fascist state and sent military assistance to Franco.

It was also in this year of dangerous international conflicts that Hitler made his carefully timed decision to drive the French out of the Rhineland and bring that territory back to the Reich. In March, 1936, German troops moved into the Rhineland and occupied it without any armed resistance from the French. When the National Socialist government began its campaign for "re-election" in Germany in 1936, it could point to Germany's active engagement in various crucial international developments, all of which were favorable to the nation's heroic image. Hitler won an overwhelming victory. However, when he claimed 98 per cent of the vote, the figure was looked upon with suspicion in Germany as well as abroad; there arose the famous political joke among Germans that wherever one turned one was confronted with those 2 per cent.

Despite this joke, Hitler was at the peak of his popularity in Germany. In July, 1936, he signed a treaty with Austria to improve relations between the two countries. The fact that the Olympic Games were to be held in Berlin gave a great boost to German prestige. The games began on August 1, 1936, and thousands of foreigners attended.

With the growing power of the party and the increasing prestige of the National Socialist government, the party congresses became each year more elaborate. In 1936, an increased number of diplomatic delegations attended, although England, France, and the United States still did not send observers. Dr. Ley had invited a hundred business leaders to participate in this rally. They were lodged in the huge hall of a restaurant that had been subdivided into small cubicles; each was equipped with a bed, a closet, and a small table, and there were zippered curtains to ensure the occupants' privacy. For the convenience of the businessmen, offices were set up where they could keep in touch with their work.[1]

On Tuesday, September 8, 110 historic flags of the army and navy were brought to the city to mark the opening of the Party Day. In the afternoon, an infantry battalion marched through the streets carrying the old flags. They were exhibited in the camp grounds of the armed forces.[2] (For the rally visitors, an exhibition of banners and uniforms was shown at a local museum. On display were all official German flags, and the various National Socialist uniforms since 1925.)[3]

At 3:30 P.M., Hitler arrived by train from Berchtesgaden. He was met by Streicher, Liebel, Dr. Ley, and his special honor guards.

Since early afternoon, thousands of people had been waiting for his arrival. Two long lines of Hitler Youth linked hands on each side of the road to hold back the spectators. The large crowds cheered as his car drove slowly to the Deutscher Hof, where he later came to a balcony to thank the people for their welcome.[4] At 6:00 P.M., the official welcoming ceremony was held at the Town Hall. Hitler arrived with Hess, Liebel, Streicher, Himmler, Dietrich, Brueckner, and Schwab. Fanfares announced their arrival, but the waiting guests greeted Hitler silently. Mayor Liebel welcomed him in the name of the city and presented him with a 400-year-old drawing of the defense plans of the old city of Nuremberg. Hitler accepted the gift and thanked the city in a brief address.[5] That night, he went to a special performance of *Die Meistersinger von Nürnberg,* given at the Opera for himself and high members of the government.[6]

Not even the higher echelon of the party knew what new doctrines might be announced at the rally. When well-informed Nazis were questioned by correspondents in their hotel lobbies that evening, they admitted they had no idea what plans Hitler had for the convention.[7] At the annual reception for the international press in the Kulturvereinshaus, the appearance of Ernst Hanfstaengl caused a mild sensation; it had been rumored that he had been removed from his high position and that he had come to the rally as a private individual. The matter was put to Hanfstaengl himself. "Humbug," he said. "I am here, am I not?"[8]

A drizzling rain drenched the participants on their way to the Luitpold Hall for the first session of the congress on Wednesday morning. Hitler and the high party officials arrived, and were welcomed in the usual ceremonies. Rudolf Hess officially opened the congress, as he had in previous years. This year, he strongly denounced the political chaos in Spain. Adolf Wagner then read Hitler's annual proclamation to the delegates. The opening emphasized that the soundness of National Socialist principles had been proved by their success. This rally was to be called the Party Day of Honor and Freedom, and these two ideas were to dominate all its meetings and activities.[9]

The new party program for the next four years was announced. It stressed the desire for peace; Hitler rejected war for any purpose save to vindicate German national honor. The proclamation also listed the achievements of four years of Nazi rule. Hitler said that in January, 1933, when he had asked for four years in which to attain his goals, his enemies had prophesied that the National Socialists would not remain in power six weeks. They would have laughed, he boasted, if he had set forth as a program what had actually been achieved. The proclamation also contained a bitter attack on Bolshevism, which Hitler said represented only one of the many facets of the international Jewish conspiracy to undermine world order.

The New York Times reported that all of these points were enthusiastically acclaimed by the audience. The loudest cheering greeted the declaration concerning the colonies (which listeners took to be an indication that Germany would seek more territory in the future) and the statement that the goals set by the Nazis had been achieved—without the presence of a single Jew in the national leadership.

Hitler's speech Wednesday night in the Opera House to the delegates of the cultural meeting repeated the ideas of the proclamation; it was a diatribe against Bolshevism and Judaism.[10] One of the highlights of the meeting was the announcement that prizes would be awarded for outstanding achievements in the arts and sciences. Since Germans were no longer allowed to accept a Nobel Prize, the National Socialists had created their own rewards. On this occasion, Rosenberg announced the awarding of a prize in art to Heinrich Anacker, a Storm Trooper who had recorded the struggle of the movement in poetry and song. A prize in science went to Professor Philipp Lenard of Heidelberg University.

The third day of the rally was devoted to the Labor Service. A parade was held in the Zeppelinwiese, which had been enlarged and altered since the previous rally. It now covered an area of 90,000 square meters and was capable of holding 250,000 men; the number of seats for spectators had also been increased from 50,000 to 70,000. With knapsacks and blankets on their backs, and spades on their shoulders, 90,000 picked men of the corps paraded before Hitler in the arena. Although the men represented only one-tenth of the German Labor Service, the whole organization celebrated. Radio broadcasts across the country carried the commands spoken on the Zeppelinwiese, and the labor men sang and marched as though they, too, were in the show at Nuremberg.[11]

The sky was gray and threatening when Hitler arrived at the Stadium, but in spite of the weather the stands were filled to capacity.[12] A company of buglers and drummers at the front of the tribune signaled Hitler's arrival, and the people rose and cheered him. Immediately the Labor Service began its march before Hitler, who stood in his car and took the salute as the regiments passed him. Except for the fact that they did not have rifles and ammunition belts, the marchers could not be distinguished from regular troops, *The New York Times* reported. Their spades on their shoulders, the men marched for one and a half hours. Six of the eight battalions were accompanied by bands, the other two sang; these last two were capless and stripped to the waist, for they were parading during working hours. Behind the men came the massed banners of the Labor Service.

It was during this rally that the Labor Service men performed a new Nazi ritual—one typical of the party's attempts to create a pseudo-religious cult as a substitute for Christian worship.[13] The regiments held their spades at "present arms" and then stood at attention. From a loudspeaker in the center of the grandstand, a clear voice sounded over the field: "Once a year the spade shall rest. Once a year there comes for us the time to stand before our Fuehrer, for whom we work day by day. In this hour, new faith is kindled."

"We are ready," responded the regiments in chorus.

After the whole assembly had sung a song, the voice again chanted: "No one is too good . . . ," and the men, standing with their hands clasped on their grounded spades, completed the sentence: ". . . to work for Germany."

"No one is too humble . . . ," chanted the voice—". . . to work for Germany," came the response from the ranks again.

"Each has the right and each has the duty," proclaimed the voice. And again the chorus repeated the refrain, ". . . to work for Germany, the Fatherland."

From the ranks came a new voice: "We have carried you deep in our hearts, but we cannot say it in words."

"Germany, Fatherland," chanted the chorus.

The voice continued: "Then the law came, work became duty. Now we all stand side by side."

"Germany, Fatherland," came the response.

"The fulfillment of duty for us is not serfdom. We carry the spade in the service of the nation. We come before you as workers," chanted the voice.

"Germany, Fatherland," answered the chorus once again.

"The Fuehrer wants to give the world peace."

"Wherever he leads, we follow," responded the Labor Service men.

They joined in another song, and then the voice took up its chant again: "We lift up our heads and think of our brothers who suffered in the trenches, and of the others who fought murder and hatred in the streets. They died for Germany."

And the chorus responded: "But today we can live for Germany."

The structure of the chanting and the response are obviously an imitation of church ritual. The party leadership consciously increased the mystical and religious aspects of the Nazi ceremonies.[14]

Following this ceremony, Konstantin Hierl briefly addressed the Labor Service, expressing, he said, the pride the men felt marching and performing before their leader. Hitler then addressed the men; he told of his great satisfaction and pride in the Labor Service and their work and once again recited the long list of his administration's achievements since the seizure of power. The ceremonies ended with a parade of the Labor Service through the streets of Nuremberg.

At the afternoon session of the congress, Alfred Rosenberg and Josef Goebbels addressed the delegates. Both attacked Judaism and Bolshevism.[15] *The New York Times* reported that the people of Nuremberg were seriously frightened when a number of planes flew low over the city early the next morning; after Goebbels' ranting against Bolshevism, they feared that the Russians were attacking while the Nazis were all together in one town. In fact, the planes had flown in for Monday's grand military demonstration. Newspaper correspondents were not told the number of planes or their classification, but reporters estimated that there were about 400 of them, chiefly medium-heavy bombers and fighter planes.[16]

An anti-Bolshevik propaganda exhibition was displayed on a train, which was later to travel to cities and villages all over Germany. The train consisted of twelve cars; each carried a large painted sign reading: "Bolshevism—World Enemy Number 1." A wall of one room was covered with photographs of the Soviet leaders. The photographs had been retouched to give the men a sinister appearance. There were battered rifles and machine guns seized in Munich after the Communist uprising in 1919, facsimiles of Bolshevik orders and proclamations of that time, and many huge photographs of the corpses of "the victims of Bolshevik rule," of starving Russian children, and of the horrors associated with the early Soviet government.[17]

There were also samples of Russian textiles and domestic products, which were clearly inferior to the German articles exhibited. *The New York Times* commented that a steady stream of visitors filed through the rooms, and that if not profitable, the exhibit was probably at least self-supporting.[18]

On September 11, the fourth day of the rally, the women's division of the party met in the Congress Hall. The anti-Bolshevik propaganda was continued.[19] Mrs. Scholtz-Klink spoke on Bolshevik evils and failures from the feminine point of view. The most promising theories in life, she proposed, were likely to be the greatest practical failures. To show this, she spoke of what had happened to women in Russia. A Soviet law passed in November, 1920, had given Russian women equality with men—the same right to work, the same duty to provide for themselves, and the same right over their bodies, including the right to birth control. She described how marriage procedures had been simplified, and how divorce was provided at will. But at the same time, she said, women had been put to work in heavy industry, and girls as well as boys trained in the use of arms; the Red Army was the only army in the world that prepared women for actual fighting. The results, she said, were abandoned, sick, or overworked women, unhappy and neglected children, and a rapid reduction in the birth rate. The Soviet government had been forced to moderate its laws the previous June. This, said Mrs. Scholtz-Klink, was life's answer to theories that treated human beings as though they were automatons. She expressed the desire that the truly national women of Germany, as the mothers of their country, should unite in a strong demonstration against such evils.

Hitler attended this meeting and afterwards briefly addressed the women delegates.[20]

In the evening, the main event of the day took place: the meeting of the political leaders.[21] When darkness descended, 140,000 Gauleiters assembled in the Zeppelinwiese to hear Hitler's address. They stood in long rows, facing the grandstand. Narrow lanes were left between the rows of men; at the center, a wide aisle was left open. *The New York Times'* correspondent, who described the scene as "even more beautiful and impressive than any that had gone before," gave the following account of the evening's events:

At 8:30 a trumpet fanfare following a roar of cheers outside the arena constantly coming nearer announced Hitler's arrival. Then he appeared, a lone figure atop the wide steps at the far side of the arena, where the wide lane ended. Awaiting him on the steps was a great gathering of high Nazi officials, all, like himself, in brown uniform.

As he appeared there shone upward from a hidden circle of 150 army searchlights behind the grandstands as many spears of light to the central point above. It was the same device employed at the closing ceremony of the Olympic Games, but it was greatly improved and infinitely larger.

In this bright light Hitler walked down the steps through the group awaiting him and slowly a procession with him at the head marched across the field to the tribune. The thunderous cheers quite drowned the music of the massed bands playing him in.

He ascended the tribune and stood there waiting until there was complete silence. Then suddenly there appeared far in the distance a mass of advancing red color. It was the 25,000 banners of Nazi organizations in all parts of Germany.

The color bearers marched with them across the rear of the brown columns on the field. Then they came forward, six abreast in the narrower lanes and twenty abreast in the wide center aisle, so there was presented the spectacle of a great tide of crimson seeping through the lanes between the solid blocs of brown.

Simultaneously the minor searchlights along the pillared rim above the grandstands were turned down on the field, lighting up the gilded eagles on the standards, so the flood of red was flecked with gold. The effect was indescribably beautiful.*

Dr. Robert Ley, the leader of the Labor Front, introduced Hitler. Hitler's strident voice filled the arena, echoing through loudspeakers. In a highly emotional speech, he praised the progress that had been made in the last three years, and conjured up before his audience muddled and melodramatic visions of a grand Teutonic future.

* This excerpt (*The New York Times* of September 12, 1936) is typical of that paper's coverage of the Party Days in the years 1933–38. The *Times'* correspondent was clearly deeply impressed by the rallies, and his reports were almost devoid of criticism.

The following day (September 12) was the Day of the Hitler Youth. Gathered in the Stadium next to the Zeppelinwiese were 47,000 Hitler Youths, both boys and girls, between the ages of twelve and eighteen—the largest number of Hitler Youth ever assembled.[22] Hitler reviewed the battalions with Rudolf Hess, his deputy party leader, and Baldur von Schirach, the leader of the Hitler Youth. He then made a brief speech in which he told them that they embodied Germany's fondest hopes. He said that the old guard that had built up the Reich was already aging, and one day, from the strain of battle and sorrow, would have to pass on. The new Germany would then have to rely on the new generation; he was confident, he said, that they would grow up worthy of their fathers and brothers who had fought in the last war. The assembled boys and girls were an impressive spectacle, *The New York Times'* reporter wrote. The boys were in brown shirts, the girls in white shirts, and the naval contingents in blue shirts and jackets of brown velvet. With their pink, healthy faces and blond hair, the correspondent wrote, the gathering resembled a huge flowerbed.[23]

The afternoon was devoted to the Labor Front. During the meeting in the Congress Hall, several ominous remarks were made by high party officials.[24] Hitler then spoke informally on the difference between Russia under Bolshevik rule and Germany under National Socialism. The social and economic disorders in Russia had sometimes been explained by the fact that she had been through a war and a revolution. Yet Germany, too, had experienced a war and undergone a revolution, Hitler said. The difference was that he had made it a fundamental principle not to destroy anything. He added that additional work for the unemployed was necessary to increase every man's share in consumer goods. He asserted that wages were not based on production, but that production itself was a wage. If he had wanted to, he said, he could have substituted commissars for employers, as the Bolsheviks had done in Russia, but he had preferred to establish an economic democracy. But, in his opinion, things should not drift as they please in a democracy. Economic principles should come first. Also, the people of young Germany should be better educated; the Labor Front could play a great role in this. Hitler ridiculed Russia for not having achieved as much as the Germans. He noted sarcastically that the Russians had invited members of the international diplomatic corps to the opening of their eleven-kilometer subway, at a time when 7,000 kilometers of highway were being built in Germany.

He contrasted Germany's shortage of land with Soviet Russia's great wealth of territory. He pointed out that Russia was eighteen times the size of Germany, yet the Bolsheviks could not feed their people:

> How Germany has to work to wrest a few square kilometers from the ocean and from the swamps, while others are swimming in superfluity of land—if I had the Ural Mountains, with their incalculable stores of treasures in raw materials, Siberia, with its vast forests, and the Ukraine, with its tremendous wheat fields, Germany under the National Socialist leadership would swim in plenty.

He defended the feasibility of his new Four-Year Plan. He promised his audience that his new plans would eliminate the present shortage of cotton, and that within the next four years Germany would produce its own cloth. Within the same period, new factories would make Germany independent of the international rubber market. He promised to produce synthetic fuel for automobiles from the oil and coal available to Germany.

The following day was devoted to the traditional Storm Troopers' review and to Hitler's press conference.[25] The brown-clad battalions and the SS contingents in their black uniforms rallied in the Luitpold Arena from 8:00 A.M. until 4:00 P.M. *The New York Times'* correspondent wrote of these ceremonies:

> Like preceding demonstrations of National Socialist strength, of which this was the climax before the army's own field day tomorrow, today's was a spectacle calculated to remain in the memory of all beholders. No country in Europe—it may even be said, no country in the world—could duplicate its significance, for it demonstrated the almost limitless reservoir of militant manhood, hardened and drilled and devoted to the point of fanaticism to Germany and the regime that rules it. Fifty-five thousand Storm Troopers, 20,000 Schutz-Staffel men, 10,000 Motor Corps men, and 26,000 aviators from uniformed sports organizations outside the army formed the parading body. More than 100,000 additional Storm Troopers, standing shoulder to shoulder, lined the miles of streets through which they passed and kept back from the roadways the hundreds

of thousands of spectators. All these men went on duty at 5 o'clock in the morning. By 8 o'clock the street guards were in position and the paraders were massed on open ground adjoining the Zeppelin field and stadium. It was an impressive sight.[26]

Before Hitler mounted the speakers' platform, the loudspeakers ordered complete silence. Within seconds, there was absolute quiet. In this cathedral-like atmosphere, Hitler addressed his followers. He said that their singling him out among millions to be their leader was a miracle, and that he had found such loyal followers was his good fortune. He reminded them of the promise he had given them four years ago and rhetorically asked them whether he had kept it. The high point of his speech was a list of party achievements since the seizure of power. He pointed out that the party's followers in Germany now numbered in the millions, and that they all would stand against the country's infiltration by international Communism. At this meeting, the traditional ritual in honor of the party dead was also solemnly performed.[27]

At noon, Hitler gave a luncheon party in a luxurious suite in the Nuremberg castle for a few special guests and a small number of foreign correspondents. Before the luncheon, Hitler discussed the historic surroundings with his guests. He also commented proudly on the morning's demonstrations and on the devotion of his followers. When asked for an estimate of the strength of his active followers, he placed the total number of political leaders at about 2.8 million, including district leaders and Storm Troopers. *The New York Times'* correspondent wrote that Hitler's face showed the strain of six day of public appearances, but that as soon as the conversation touched on a theme that interested him, he was able to shake off his weariness and engage in discussion with vehemence and fervor. He said he was highly amused by the idea that the rallies at Nuremberg were camouflaged training grounds for German mobilization. He called the idea absurd, because in his opinion there was no connection between a gathering like this in a city inside the country and sending troops to a frontier 400 kilometers long. When the correspondents expressed admiration for the spirit of loyalty conveyed during the demonstrations, Hitler answered that if he wanted to, he could organize a real demonstration against Communism by simply giving a free hand to his propaganda machine—in response to that, his sup-

porters would come by the millions. He launched out against Bolshevism, but then swiftly changed his tone and the subject, and
invited his guests to join him at lunch.[28]

After lunch, Hitler was driven to the large square before the
Town Hall and stood for more than three hours in his car reviewing the Storm Troopers. The march, which had become a traditional highlight of the rallies, was bigger this year than ever before.

The last day of the rally was devoted to the army, which had
gained considerably in prestige since the occupation of the Rhineland. Under the supervision of military experts selected by Hitler,
the army had been going through a process of modernization.
Even the old name of the army, the Reichswehr, had been changed
to the Wehrmacht, a term that sounded new and modern yet
evoked the Germanic past so much romanticized by the National
Socialists.

The day began with the traditional maneuvers on the Zeppelinwiese before hundreds of thousands of spectators and party dignitaries. The German army and air force, with a single brigade of
blue jackets to represent the navy, provided the air force pageant.
The huge dirigible *Hindenburg* hovered over the battle area. The
show closed with a parade of troops of all services.

The military day, with its display of national strength, was
planned to provide an impressive climax to the rally. *The New York
Times'* correspondent wrote that the modernized German army
was a worthy descendant of the army of World War I. The correspondent's impression was that, just as in 1914 the Imperial army
had entered the war better prepared than any other nation, Hitler's
military apparatus in 1936 was better adapted to the conditions of
modern warfare than that of any other country.[29] The observers
were most surprised by the degree of motorization. Fully half of
the infantry that passed before Hitler was motorized. Each cavalry
regiment included a machine-gun company that dismounted and
went into action within a few seconds, and at its rear was a section
of light, quick-firing guns to reinforce the cavalry and machine
guns.

There was also an impressive anti-aircraft demonstration. Batteries of light and heavy guns entered the arena at high speeds; in
less than two minutes, the guns were set up and firing almost with
the rapidity of machine guns. The guns swung about simultane-

ously, sweeping areas with great precision. Having theoretically repulsed the attacking aircraft, the men re-mounted their guns and left just as speedily. The whole action was begun, fought, and finished, and the arena cleared, within sixteen minutes. It struck foreign visitors as an amazing demonstration of the speed of modern warfare.

The infantry then set up a line of barbed-wire entanglements and established defensive lines behind it; they were then attacked by motorized infantry who came in on mounted, armored, six-wheeled cars. The attackers were beaten off, so they were reinforced by a motorcycle company with machine guns; when the positions still could not be taken, the defenders were finally ousted by a battalion of light tanks that crashed through the wire and spread a smoke screen, from behind which the infantry fought their way through with hand grenades. The cavalry had not only charged against the infantry, but showed how it would operate in conjunction with armored cars as the advance guard of a movement. There was also a demonstration to show how motorcycle units and armored cars with machine guns operating through their turrets could be used instead of cavalry as scouting and advance parties. With the anti-aircraft batteries, field guns, and howitzers, went armored radio cars, whose crews raised telescopic masts, rigged antennae, and established communication with amazing speed.[30]

Despite the seeming perfection of the demonstrations, there was at least one observer who noted mishaps. Stephen H. Roberts relates:

> But even on a billiard table surface things could not go according to plan. The machine gun nearest Hitler jammed; one of the two-men tanks dropped a piece of its armor; and there were many little confusions. It was odd to see the advancing infantry men flinging themselves on the ground, not naturally but in so many precise movements as on a parade ground. For hours that afternoon Nuremberg had all the experiences of a war, except for the ambulances and the burying squads. A rally has no time for that side of war.[31]

Every part of the demonstration brought out something new in warfare or new adaptations of old practices. Even the goose step used by the infantry and ground regiments of the air force had been changed. Since the old step was difficult to maintain in the close ranks that paraded at the rallies, a new step was substituted, called the "kick step," in which the boot was not raised quite so high nor extended so far. Irreverent foreigners, seeing this less imposing pace for the first time, dubbed it the "chicken step."[32]

Only 18,000 officers and men took part in these "defense demonstrations," as the exhibition was officially called. Included were a regiment of infantry, two of cavalry, four batteries of field artillery (both heavy and light), two anti-aircraft sections, a motorized infantry battalion, a motorcycle-and-machine-gun company, a battalion of whippet tanks, four regiments of the air force, a ground force, and anti-aircraft men. It was apparent that the air force on parade equaled the number of infantrymen and cavalry together.

Perhaps more striking than any of these was the display of aircraft, although it was not as extensive as some had expected. Altogether there were 374 planes in the air—233 biplanes and 141 monoplanes. The biplanes were fast scout and pursuit machines; the monoplanes were bombers and heavy fighters. They flew past Hitler and later maneuvered in squadrons of twenty-seven planes, each with three V-shaped formations of nine planes. Three squadrons composed a larger group, known as Geschwader, to which were added three planes for leaders—that is, eighty-four planes in all.

The planes flew before the tribune in salute, then executed a series of maneuvers that ended with a dive by each plane from a great height nearly to the level of the platform where Hitler stood. Afterward, the squadrons staged a series of sham battles. Finally a group of three, simulating an attack force, attempted to bomb the anti-aircraft batteries that had dashed in to meet them. They were repelled first at low level by light, quick fire, then at a higher level by heavier guns. The noise of this battle was deafening. In the midst of the demonstration, *The New York Times* reported, one foreign correspondent remarked: "Please page the Treaty of Versailles."

The entire aircraft demonstration lasted almost half an hour. It was followed by cavalry maneuvers that produced the highest praise from the audience and press for Germany's cavalry. Then the motorized infantry regiment staged a sham battle against a line of sharpshooters. The armored cars ran forward and backward with almost equal ease. A remarkable system, using colored

discs to signal, directed the operation. When their turn came, the
tanks advanced to the arena and divided into two columns, which
circled the arena and halted before Hitler. A white flag flashed
from the leading tank, in which the commander rode. Similar
flags, in the hands of the commanders of the other two, answered
it, and suddenly the doors of the turrets and motor enclosures of
every car sprang open, and the driver and machine gunners, in
their black berets and loose-fitting uniforms, stood at salute at
each side of the tanks.

Visitors at the rally were not unimpressed by the beauty of the
carefully rehearsed demonstrations. They were, nevertheless, very
much aware of the new aggressiveness and belligerency of the
speeches, particularly Hitler's.[33]

Later in the day, Hitler addressed the closing session of the congress. In the opinion of *The New York Times'* correspondent, the
Chancellor's speech was an anticlimax after "the sound and fury
of the last seven days." It seemed to exude "hope for peace, pride
in National Socialist accomplishments, and confidence in Germany's future." It was, the correspondent wrote, "a speech of the
Hitler who sometimes dreams aloud. . . ." Hitler made no reference to international affairs, nor to the future course of Germany's
foreign policy. He denounced Bolshevism, but called for no action
against it, and made the usual nationalistic and anti-Semitic remarks.[34]

On the evening of this eventful day—which, with its rattling of
armor, had made many foreign observers uneasy—the SA bands
gathered under Hitler's windows and serenaded him with his favorite marches and with taps, as they had done on the last evening
of the earlier rallies.

The reaction of the world press to this spectacular week of mass
demonstrations, modern war games, and continual political harangues, was mixed. The London *Times* felt that the tone of the
proclamation suggested that the Nazis were so preoccupied with
the Bolshevik bogy in foreign affairs that there would be a relaxa-
tion of the pressure militant Nazi activity had been exerting at
home.

Both the Roman Catholic and the Protestant churches will pre-
sumably benefit by this concentration on foreign affairs. Even the
Jews may find themselves no worse off for some little time to come,

although the wild cheering which greeted a casual but unfavorable reference to the Jews in the proclamation today, was an indication of the extent to which an announcement of further anti-Jewish legislation would have been welcomed in extremist party circles.[35]

On September 15, *The Times* commented further on the violent anti-Bolshevik tone of Hitler's speech to the closing session of the congress, when he gave a stern warning to all Europe against the Bolshevik menace. Hitler had declared that National Socialism could not enter into any kind of bargaining with Bolshevism, and that the Germans could never negotiate with the Bolsheviks. The reporter felt that a sensation of relief would go through Europe after the week of rallies in Nuremberg was concluded. He felt that although Hitler had repeatedly stressed his willingness to preserve the peace, he had actually begun to sow seeds of unrest with his belligerency toward Russia.

The Italian papers, as usual, gave very detailed reports on the events in Nuremberg. All the major speeches were translated. The French papers also gave extensive coverage of the rallies, especially the army maneuvers and Hitler's final speech before the congress. The Soviet press commented sharply on Hitler's references to the Urals, Siberia, and the Ukraine: "We know now the modest dreams of Mr. Hitler. But they are vain. As easily could the promoters of the Nuremberg circus see their own ears as our territory. The Soviets are strong and prepared. When the time comes it will provide a bitter disappointment for those who suffer such hysterical dreams."[36]

The 1936 party congress had been the largest and most lavish display to date of Nazi power and solidarity. "At Nuremberg, in September, the party rally, which lasted a week, was on a scale which even Nazi pageantry had never before equalled. Germany's new masters entertained with a splendor that rivaled that of the displays of Le Roi Soleil and the Czars of Russia."[37] In addition to promoting their regime both inside and outside Germany with pageantry and demagoguery, the government used this show-case to harangue the world with its dominant theme of the year: anti-Bolshevism. At the same time, it paraded before the astonished eyes of Europe an army that had shaken off the fetters of the Versailles Treaty and become one of the world's most modern instruments of war.

13   THE PARTY DAY OF LABOR
1937

The year 1936–37 was the peak of the four-year period of uninter-
rupted national growth under the National Socialist government.
Although these years of political and economic success established
Hitler's prestige in Germany and abroad, the motivation for this
laudable effort was not what it appeared to be: Hitler did not conceive a solid economy to provide higher living standards for Germany, but to serve as a basis for a gigantic war machine.

Part of this power scheme, undoubtedly, was the effort to establish firmer ties between Berlin and Rome; attempts at this went
on from September, 1936, to September, 1937. During this period,
the most influential spokesmen of both governments met for fre-
quent consultations: Goering was sent to Rome in January, 1937,
Neurath in May, War Minister Werner von Blomberg in June,
and Joachim von Ribbentrop in October. There is no question

that the initiative came from Berlin, for Hitler was anxiously
watching the attempts of the British and French to renew friendly
relations with the Duce.

On January 30, 1937, the Nazis celebrated the fourth anniversary of their seizure of power. In a speech before the Reichstag,
Hitler sharply demanded the return of Germany's colonies and
expressed concern over the plight of the German minorities in foreign countries. Under the new Four-Year-Plan, the German economy continued to expand. The purposes of the Plan were to
overcome the shortage of raw materials and to maintain, if not
increase, the present pace of rearmament. As a further step toward
strengthening the national economy, the German-Polish economic
pact was renewed for another two years in February, 1937. In
Spain, the ferocious Civil War went into its second phase. On
May 30, Spanish Loyalist planes bombed the German cruiser
Deutschland, which participated in the international sea control,
and twenty of the crew were killed. As a retaliatory measure, German battleships shelled the fortifications of the harbor of Almería
the next day.

Hitler's position as party chief and national leader was completely
secure by the fall of 1937. He was at the peak of his popularity;
he had won the Germans' almost blind confidence by having
convinced them for four years that a better life for all was the
party's ultimate goal. The coming years were to show that this was
not so—in fact, to show to the world that Hitler's most striking
achievement in those four years had been to hypnotize the German people into this blind faith and obedience.

The preparations for the 1937 rally began on July 1 of that
year. The well-trained organizing team was once again set in motion. The preparations were the same each year, but the process
became more and more streamlined, and the realization of each
rally's blueprint increasingly efficient.

Some small innovations were made to improve the events. Preparations were made to record the entire rally proceedings.[1] The
anti-Bolshevik exhibition of the previous years was presented
again, but it had been enlarged and was set up in a permanent
building, the former home of the Transport Ministry. In the entrance hall was a globe twelve yards in circumference. Through

intricate electrical wiring, small "fires" could be seen breaking out in countries threatened by Bolshevism. Two rooms were dedicated to the victory of Italian Fascism over Bolshevism. In the opening ceremony, Julius Streicher dedicated the exhibition to the hundreds of thousands of visitors from Germany and abroad. Among the speakers was General Alessandro Melchiori, the representative of Dino Alfieri, the Italian Minister of Press and Propaganda. In his speech, he paid tribute to the 1,200 Italian Black Shirts who had died in the fight against Communism.[2]

As in previous years, Nuremberg assumed a festive appearance for the rally. By now a routine had been established for decorating the city and for feeding and housing the masses of visitors. The preparations ran smoothly; the beautiful old city was once again squeezed into its Nazi uniform, and 3.5 million mess kits were carted into the thirteen tent cities on the periphery of the rally grounds.[3]

For the first time, the diplomatic corps of most of the Western world attended the congress. Among the visitors were Prentiss Gilbert, the United States Chargé d'Affaires, representing Ambassador William E. Dodd; Sir Nevile Henderson, the British Ambassador; and André François-Poncet, the French Ambassador. Four conspicuous absentees were the papal nuncio, the Russians, the Norwegians, and the Peruvians (who were said to be nursing a grievance over a soccer incident during the 1936 Olympics). The American, British, Greek, Chinese, Danish, Swedish, Egyptian, Dutch, Czechoslovak, and Belgian envoys came to Nuremberg by special train, on which they lived during the rally.

Benito Mussolini did not attend the rally (although a week later he came to Germany for talks with Hitler). Japan's Prince Chichibu, brother of the emperor, and General Franco's brother Nicolas were the guests of honor. Chichibu had come because he was particularly interested in the exercises of the new German army.

When Hitler arrived on September 6, the eve of the rally, the picture was the same as in previous years. The city's decorated streets were filled with throngs eager to catch a glimpse of him as he was welcomed by a group of dignitaries. According to the custom of the former rallies, all the church bells of Nuremberg rang for a half hour to mark the beginning of the Party Days. The official welcoming ceremony, with the usual fanfare, speeches, and anthems,[4] took place at the Town Hall, and late in the afternoon Otto Dietrich was host at a reception for the press.[5]

On September 7, the congress was opened with the reading of Hitler's proclamation.[6] The 1937 proclamation appealed to the nation to increase its economic and industrial efforts and so ensure a prosperous and secure future, but it held little promise for immediate improvements in living conditions. For the moment, the people were to tighten their belts and accept the existing wage scale. The proclamation voiced a strong claim for the repossession of Germany's colonial territories and expressed indignation at the Allies' attitude on this issue. It contained the usual attacks on Judaism and Bolshevism.

At the end of the proclamation, which took a full hour to read, came the long-awaited declaration on foreign policy. There were three terse points: the Treaty of Versailles is dead; Germany is free; the guarantee of our liberty is our army.[7] Thus Hitler unilaterally dissolved the agreement Germany had entered into with the Allies after the war.

Hitler made his first long speech later in the evening at the annual cultural session at the Opera House.[8] For an hour and a half, before a crowded house, he spoke on the influence of art on humanity and, in particular, on the German people. The *Times* reported that Hitler was frequently and enthusiastically applauded, but that his words were often "so mystical or so involved" that listeners were unsure of his argument. He did not mention Bolshevism, Marxism, or the Jews specifically, but it was clear that his criticism of trends in modern art was directed mainly against the Jews, who were extremely active in this field.

Josef Goebbels followed Hitler as the second speaker. He said that the award of a 1935 Nobel Prize to Karl von Ossietzky, a pacifist and a declared foe of Nazism, had been a flagrant insult to the German government. Hitler had subsequently issued an order forbidding any German to accept the Nobel Prize in the future. Instead, the German national prizes were awarded at the rallies. This year, the architect Ludwig Troost and the surgeon August Bier were recipients of prizes. The third recipient was the distinguished surgeon Ferdinand Sauerbruch. The fourth recipient was Wilhelm Flichner, an explorer who had been missing for two years in Central Asia, and who had returned to Germany only a few days before.

The next day, September 8, was devoted to the Labor Service. The activities, the mass meetings, and the show marching were conducted as in previous years.[9] The ritual of choruses and individual voices chanting ideological slogans, which was initiated at the 1936 Labor Service Day, was repeated. The speeches contained the usual propaganda. The only addition this year was the Women's Labor Service Corps, which attended the Labor Service Day exercises for the first time. Unlike the men's corps, the Women's Labor Service was voluntary. Girls were permitted to join at eighteen, and they remained in the corps for two years. They were usually assigned to farms that were short of help.

On September 9, a huge crowd witnessed the laying of the cornerstone for the gigantic new sports stadium (capacity: 250,000). An impressive setting had been devised for this ceremony. Around the temporary grandstands were 2,000 Nazi banners, one from each district in the country. Massed in the center were the crimson and gold standards of the districts, surmounted by eagles. There were present 18,000 members of the nation's military and semimilitary organizations, in their uniforms of brown, black, dark blue, gray, and green. The army, navy, air force, Labor Service, special guards, Hitler Youth, political leaders, and police were represented. *The New York Times* wrote that from above, this mass of men and banners resembled a huge tulip field.[10]

At the congress meeting later in the afternoon, Goebbels denounced Bolshevism. His denunciation was as sweeping and vituperative as usual, and largely followed the lines of a similar speech he had made the year before. He made his usual appeal to the nations of Europe to fight against Bolshevism before it was too late.

Otto Dietrich, the press chief, once again criticized the institution of the free press as the democratic countries understood it. He said that a powerless government does not dare declare war on the destructive powers of the press, because its existence depends on the press. So until the advent of National Socialism, the world remained blind to the true enemy of peace, the greatest and most dangerous warmonger of the age—the anonymous power of the press, which poisoned public opinion throughout the world. Censorship, according to Dietrich, was really the invention of a pope, who had introduced it to Germany. He quoted Frederick the Great, who had said that since freedom of the press was always abused, control was necessary. He also cited French legislators who had denounced their press after the Revolution had freed it.

Such were the first sweet blossoms on the tree of the freedom of the press, said Dietrich. In his view, the freedom of the British press was a mere deception; the American press was only a number of business enterprises that tried to meet the masses' demand for sensation. He said that a leading American newspaper proprietor (whom he did not name) had admitted this. He concluded his speech with the admonition: "We can afford to speak frankly and take the bull by the horns, for we long ago cleansed our press of all elements of decay, of liars, of agitators and material muzzling of the spirit. Do likewise and you will experience a miracle."[11]

That night rain marred a huge torchlight procession of political leaders and Storm Troopers who paraded past Hitler's hotel.

On the following day (September 10), visiting diplomats were treated to lunch at the castle and a sightseeing tour of Nuremberg, during which they saw the various construction projects underway for future congresses. At 5:00 P.M., they were taken to the Deutscher Hof for tea with Hitler.[12]

In the afternoon, the party women, under Mrs. Scholtz-Klink, met for their annual congress in the Luitpold Hall. This year there was a record crowd of women participants. In her address to the representatives, Mrs. Scholtz-Klink set four goals for German women: to make German households conform to the exigencies of the Four-Year Plan for national self-sufficiency, to accustom German households to new products, to carry on the national anti-waste campaign, and to learn to use raw materials.[13] She said that in order to achieve these goals, 785,000 housewives were already being trained by the party in 35,000 lecture courses throughout the country. She expressed the hope that the day would not be far off when every housewife in Germany could be taught how to organize her household according to the policies of the party. Mrs. Scholtz-Klink proclaimed that woman's weapon was the soup ladle, and she told the story of the SS man's wife who had put up a sign over her husband's bed saying that this was the place where he used to sleep before he joined the SS.[14] Hitler then addressed the meeting for some thirty minutes, voicing his usual theories about women's role in the Third Reich.

At night, the political leaders met in the Zeppelinwiese for their annual ceremony. Dramatic lighting, flags, martial music, and show marching were again used to mesmerize the masses.[15] At the climax of the evening, Ley and Hitler briefly addressed the vast crowd.[16]

The following day was devoted to the Hitler Youth. All the Hitler Youths of the Langwasser camp ground were present when 104 new flags were presented to new groups. Baldur von Schirach was in charge of the ceremony. The youths stood amid the new flags singing their songs and taking part in the dedication ritual.

For the first time in the history of the rallies, Chancellor Hitler addressed a great outdoor demonstration in the rain. Except for a few hours the previous night, it had rained almost continuously during the congress. Hitler pointed out that this rainy Youth Day assembly set a precedent, and he drew a moral from it in his address to the 50,000 youths assembled in the Youth Stadium. He told them:

> It is good that for once the sun does not shine today, for we want to train people not for sunshine alone, but for stormy days. The whole education of our people would be in vain if the result was not a nation that could hold its own, even under the hardest conditions. Boys between eighteen and twenty like yourselves were once brought up for amusement only. Now we bring them up for self-denial, sacrifice, and the discipline of a healthy, hardy body.[17]

Rudolf Hess administered the oath of loyalty and obedience to the 50,000 on the field, and by this action automatically granted them party membership. (Previously, the oath had been taken in Munich, at the annual commemoration of the Munich *Putsch*.) Smaller youth assemblies all over Germany simultaneously took the oath.[18]

At Hitler's request, Goering replaced him a few hours later as principal speaker at a meeting of several thousand labor leaders in the Luitpold Hall. Hitler was present, however, and he addressed the leaders briefly, explaining that he was extremely busy and had to spare his voice because of the strain of speaking outdoors in bad weather.

Goering took the platform and extolled the virtues of the German laborers. He promised them that they would play a privileged part in the future National Socialist society. He pointed out that National Socialism had succeeded in taking the working classes away from the intellectual drivel of Marxist ideology, yet had persuaded the employers to lower class barriers and mix with the laborers.

Late that night, Heinrich Himmler invited members of the press and distinguished foreign visitors to a party on the SS camp grounds. The alleged purpose of the reception was to give guests a look at the off-duty activities of Hitler's stern elite guard.[19]

The next day was devoted to grand-scale exercises of the SA and SS. The program was the same as in earlier years: mass meetings, roll calls, flag dedications, and so on. As usual, the climax of the ceremonies was the parade of several hundred thousand Storm Troopers in downtown Nuremberg.[20]

At noon, Hitler gave a luncheon reception for the press, at which he set forth in detail his views on Germany's domestic and international situation. *The New York Times'* correspondent has given an interesting account of the gathering.[21] Hitler had made the condition that he not be directly quoted at length. Therefore the conversation proceeded rapidly, and no notes were taken. Asked whether Benito Mussolini's forthcoming visit was, in his opinion, likely to lead to an extension or reinforcement of the Rome-Berlin axis, the Chancellor replied that the visit spoke for itself. He made it clear, however, that he was inclined to view the foreign political situation with equanimity. Germany had no designs on anyone, Hitler stated. As long as Germany had remained unarmed, she had constituted a dangerous vacuum in the heart of Europe. But, he said, the vacuum was now very well filled: Hitler told his guests that Germany was now so completely absorbed in internal affairs that she had no time for "senseless adventures." He did not deny that there were difficulties, for instance, the food shortage—this, however, was the worry of the economic administrators.

Since he himself was a vegetarian by conviction and practice, he did not consider himself qualified to judge the situation, but he firmly believed that the modern food supply system was not com-

Luitpold Hall, in 1936

Review of the Hitler Youth, 1936 rally

Air maneuvers at the 1936 Army Day

Motor Corps maneuvers at the 1936 Army Day

Zeppelinwiese, in 1936

The dirigible *Hindenburg* at the army maneuvers, 1936

March past in downtown
Nuremberg, 1936

Nighttime meeting at the
1936 rally

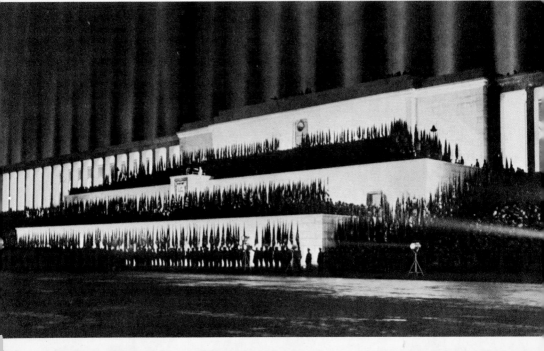

Hitler's private plane arriving from Berchtesgaden for the 1937 rally

The eternal flame at the Zeppelinwiese

March past on the Nuremberg market square, 1937 *(above)*

Hitler arriving for a reception at the Nuremberg Town Hall, 1937 *(left)*

Hitler, General von Blomberg, and Josef Goebbels viewing a sports event at the 1937 rally *(right)*

Hitler viewing the model for the German Stadium, in 1937

Day of the Labor Service, 1937

Hitler, with *(behind him, left to right)* Heinrich Himmler, Robert Ley, Rudolf Hess, and Viktor Lutze arriving at the Nuremberg railroad station for the 1938 rally

Parade of the party standards at the 1938 rally

Labor Service Day, 1938

Party standards being
carried into the Luit-
pold Hall, in 1938

Japanese delegates at the 1938 rally

Hitler with Austrian guests, 1938

Italian delegates at the 1938 rally

Hitler Youth at the 1938
rally *(left)*

Athletic exercises in the
Zeppelinwiese, 1938
(right)

Hitler Youth Day, 1938
(below)

Parade of the party standards, 1938   Eagle in the Luitpold Arena, 1938

pletely rational in any nation. In Germany it was not a question of anyone's going hungry. Others might say that Germany was only 10–12 per cent short of food and raw materials, but they forgot that such a shortage implied deprivation for 7 million Germans. He predicted a period of peace on the international scene. Germany, at least, had enough work to do at home to keep her busy for two or three decades. Among the projects he mentioned were large-scale highway construction plans and plans for extensive renewal in Berlin and Munich.

He then touched on the question of Germany's share in Europe's colonial spoils. He stressed that the Germans had an indisputable right to colonial possessions, but that this problem could be solved by common sense rather than force.

None of Hitler's speeches during the day was distinguished by new policy announcements. He reminisced about the fighting days of the movement and pointed out the great progress made by the party. Only Viktor Lutze's address sounded a new—and dangerous—note, although his remarks were brief and general. His speech contained the party's first public attack on the church and its followers in Germany. Although his threats were by no means veiled, they were extremely vague. Christians were accused of not serving their country as devotedly as they should. A good Christian was defined by Lutze as a man who served his country well.[22]

As in former years, the last day of the rally (September 13) saw a display of Germany's military prowess. The military maneuvers impressed *The New York Times'* correspondent as "pretty close to being terrifying in the efficiency of men and machines." Much new equipment was paraded: motorized infantry, motorized artillery, machine-gun battalions with motorcycles and armored cars of various types, tank regiments, anti-tank battalions equipped with guns of various calibers, searchlights, and signal and communication units. The mechanization of the new army was impressive: as a result of lessons learned in Spain, the cavalry was now only half on horseback, and half was motorized.

After the parading army contingents had cleared the field, an air-force display began. It was headed by seventeen pursuit planes that flew over the field in a swastika formation. More and more planes appeared from the low clouds in the west[23]—reconnaissance planes, bombers, fighters, and pursuit planes, flying at various heights and in different formations until the spectators felt deafened by the roar. Eighteen squadrons of Dorniers, Junkers, and Heinkels took part in the demonstration. The planes dipped low in salute over the rostrum. Meanwhile seven batteries of anti-aircraft guns sped onto the field and took up positions to repel the "attacks." It was announced that there were 1,000 men in the air and 5,000 on the ground in this demonstration. The planes returned and dove from a great height, as if bombing and machine-gunning the ground. Their dives were timed at 370 mph. When more planes came from other directions, the guns swung around to meet the new attack. It was known that perhaps one-third of the planes were equipped with the newly developed diesel engines. Following the air exercises, the signal corps gave a stunning demonstration of the modern technical devices in their equipment. One wireless truck contained a folding eighty-foot radio mast, which was hoisted and secured to the ground in three minutes and refolded and stowed away in the truck in even less time. The finale of the army maneuvers was an impressive demonstration of attack and defense exercises by two infantry contingents.

In the evening, the functionaries of the party met in the Congress Hall for the festive final session of the congress. As in the past, Wagnerian music, emotional speeches, and military displays were used to bring the rally to a rousing finish.[24] *The New York Times'* correspondent wrote about the effect that Hitler's mass hypnosis had on even the foreign correspondents during the last full party meeting.

Chancellor Adolf Hitler's final exhortation to his cohorts in the Luitpoldhalle only a few hours ago was widely broadcast for the benefit of those the hall would not hold. To every hotel lounge a loudspeaker carried his earnest tones. This hotel, temporarily taken over by working journalists, including correspondents from almost every nation, was no exception. As the cheers from the hall following the "Sieg Heil" with which he concluded died away, the hotel audience to a man and woman rose to its feet with arms raised in the Nazi salute and joined in the emotional singing of "Deutschland" followed by the Horst Wessel Lied. It was typical of the end of eight days of steadily mounting excitement that words fail adequately to describe.[25]

The apparently overwhelming effect of this macabre scene described by *The New York Times'* reporter is difficult to comprehend. The press that later professed to be unable to conceive how Hitler could have been endorsed by the German nation sent dispatches from Nuremberg hailing Germany's "historic upheaval" and speaking of Hitler's "magic spell."

The foreign press had again given the rally close coverage. English newspapers especially emphasized the events of the last day and printed a translation of Hitler's final speech to the congress; most of the headlines announced that Hitler had vowed no Communist countries would be tolerated in Europe in the future. The impressive display of army weapons received considerable attention.

Italian papers naturally devoted a great deal of space to the Nuremberg rally. For the first time, the Japanese press covered the congress extensively; it predicted a close alliance between Germany and Japan after Hitler's hospitality to Prince Chichibu.

The party pageantry reached its peak with the 1937 rally. Hitler's hold on the government was more secure than ever; the Nazi ceremonies at the rallies had been accepted for years by the nation and seemed, at this point, an unshakeable tradition. Hitler and his followers were confident that the "Thousand-Year Reich" was looking forward to another thousand rallies. Yet the 1937 rally was to be the last but one. The relative prosperity and political calm that had settled over the nation were the lull before the holocaust.

14 THE PARTY DAY OF GREATER GERMANY
1938

The year between the 1937 and 1938 rallies saw many of the crucial events that brought Europe and the world to crisis. The first
major development in Germany's international affairs followed
immediately in the wake of the 1937 Party Congress. Only a few
days after Hitler returned to Berlin from Nuremberg, Mussolini
paid him a visit. The purpose was to strengthen the Rome-Berlin
Axis. Hitler lavished on his guest all the honor and pageantry
traditionally connected with a state visit, and Mussolini was
deeply impressed by the power Hitler commanded. The two men
bestowed honorary titles on each other and intensified their
friendship, but to Mussolini the most interesting part of his visit
was an excursion to the training grounds of the German army,
where Hitler showed his guest his modern military machine. Two
months after his return to Rome, Mussolini announced Italy's
withdrawal from the League of Nations.

On the other side of the globe, Japan had launched a successful invasion of China and captured the capital of Nanking.

On March 12, 1938, German troops crossed the Austrian border and marched toward Vienna. The *Anschluss* was the Hitler government's first acquisition of territory outside the German border. Violent threats against the existing Austrian government and a forced plebiscite in Austria and Germany had brought about the takeover. Winston Churchill, who had opposed the Nazi regime from the beginning, prophesied a drastic change in the European balance of power after this brazen acquisition. Bullock sums up the strategic windfall from this move as follows:

> The acquisition of Vienna, for centuries regarded as the gateway to Southern Europe, placed the German army on the edge of the Hungarian plain and at the threshold of the Balkans. To the South, Germany now had a common frontier with Italy and Jugoslavia, no more than fifty miles from the Adriatic. To the north, Hitler was in a position to outflank Czechoslovakia's defenses and press her from three directions at once. Germany's strategic position, if Hitler was bent on a campaign of conquest, had been immeasurably improved. Nor was the contribution of Austria's economic resources in iron, steel, and magnesite to be disregarded.[1]

Shortly before the *Anschluss,* Hitler had purged the high military command of all generals who were not in complete agreement with him. In the course of this shakeup, Generals von Blomberg and von Fritzsch were removed from their positions, and Hitler gained an ever-increasing hold over the army. Less than two months after the annexation of Austria, Hitler paid a return visit to Italy. He wanted to alleviate Italian concern about his recent moves in Austria and to cement the connection between the two countries. His host gave him a reception with full state honors, and Hitler returned to Germany enthusiastic about the beauty of the Italian cities and landscape. Austria's incorporation into the Reich was soon to be followed by greatly increased terror and agitation by the Czechs in the German Sudeten district of Czechoslovakia. Hitler's propaganda machine made full use of these incidents and prepared the world for a second step across Germany's borders.

The rally of 1938—the last Nazi party congress, although its organizers and thousands of visitors from abroad did not know it—received the widest international attention. Two hundred and fifty reporters from all over the world came to cover the event. The United States and Canada sent twenty-five journalists.[2] For the first time, an American Ambassador, Hugh Wilson, attended a rally. However, the Soviet Ambassador and the papal nuncio remained in Berlin.[3] Among the visitors were 30,000 Austrians. Even Arabia sent 100 delegates.

Alerted by the experience of previous years, the party had 1,000 doctors, 1,200 nurses, and 4,000 medical assistants on duty around the clock to treat emergency cases in the 200 temporary hospitals that had been set up in the city and suburbs.[4] In order to enlist the support of intellectuals, the party invited more than one hundred leading German writers and composers to attend the rally.[5] A new and well-planned propaganda feature this year was the Strength through Joy exhibition. There were also exhibitions by leading German athletes, who donated their time and skill to promote Strength through Joy. A popular attraction for the men at the exhibition were 120 shooting galleries.[6] Every day there were concerts, vaudeville acts, puppet shows, and folk dancing to entertain the visitors.

The radio coverage was efficient and thorough, as usual. A new feature was a nightly, two-hour special program entitled "The Big Echo from Nuremberg," which broadcast highlights of the important political, cultural, and sports events of the party days.

On September 5, Otto Dietrich, the party press secretary, gave his annual reception for the 750 journalists who were covering the rally. His address was less political than in previous years, when he used to harangue the guests with Nazi contempt for freedom of the press. The major part of his speech was a flowery panegyric on National Socialism.[7]

On the same afternoon, Mayor Liebel gave the annual reception for Hitler at the Nuremberg Town Hall. The only new feature was the presentation of a replica of the Austrian crown jewels to Hitler. It is indicative of Hitler's megalomania that he had accepted Charlemagne's crown jewels one year after seizing power in Germany and now, barely six months after seizing Austria, he insisted on being presented with the insignia of the Austro-Hungarian monarchy.[8]

The official opening of the congress took place the following day. After a short address by Rudolf Hess, Adolf Wagner read

Hitler's annual proclamation. In it, Hitler warned the world not
to count on German economic difficulties; a good harvest had provided plenty of grain, allayed any fears of possible bread shortages,
and given an opportunity to create a strong reserve. The proclamation indicated that Germany had already stored up so much
food that no aggressor could use an economic blockade against her
effectively.[9] Hitler added that the Four-Year Plan, administered by
Goering, had successfully stabilized the German economy.

In the afternoon, Hess and other party leaders attended the
opening of the exhibition *"Kampf in Osten"* ("The Struggle in
the East"). Hitler had written a statement, displayed in the entrance hall, that explained the purpose of the exhibit. It stressed
the ties that held together the West European nations and said
that they were mutually dependent on each other because of
their culture, history, and future. It expressed the view that despite the wars in Europe, the Western nations not only brought
suffering and unhappiness to each other, but also exchanged ideas,
wisdom, and joy. "If we are honest with ourselves, we must admit
that we have less reason to hate than to admire each other."[10]

The first part of the exhibition illustrated the struggle of the
European nations for living space, racial purity, and fulfillment of
cultural obligations. It showed them fighting off the attacks from
the East. The second part showed the possible effects of a fight
against the East.[11] The exhibit seems to have been a move to prepare the German people for a conflict with Russia.

In the evening, party officials and special guests from all fields
of the arts assembled in the Opera for the culture congress. After
a speech by Rosenberg, which contained the usual diatribes
against Jews and Marxists, Goebbels announced the winners of
the National Prizes for Art and Science. Among them were Fritz
Todt, Ferdinand Porsche, one of the nation's foremost automobile
engineers, and Professors Willy Messerschmitt and Ernst Heinkel,
Germany's leading airplane designers. The highlight of the evening was Hitler's speech on National Socialist cultural policies,
which he said he considered to be of more lasting importance than
any other phase of the regime.

Thus far, Hitler said, National Socialist successes had been admitted in every sphere of activity except the cultural; here, international Jewry was still enforcing its "misinterpretations" upon the
world. At one moment, the world sympathized with the Jewish ex-

ponents of pseudo culture, but at the next it coolly rejected them.

Religious inspiration was alien to the National Socialist *Weltanschauung,* he asserted: "Our National Socialist architects cannot be expected to design a church, no more than one could conceive a Gothic stadium [he referred to the buildings on the rally grounds]. They cannot design a religious building, because this is incompatible with the National Socialist spirit. We have no religious buildings, we have parade grounds. To our mind, there is nothing to be gained from religious buildings."

He set up as a standard for all art its appeal to man's sense of the beautiful, the healthy, and the natural. This, he said, was in direct opposition to the Jewish belief that decadent intellectuals alone were entitled to set up standards.[12]

The next day (September 7), Labor Service Day, was marked by the usual parades and mass meetings. Once again, the visitors were thrilled by the visual effects of 40,000 spades reflecting the sunlight, a sight *The New York Times'* correspondent called "the massed glint." Hierl and Hitler briefly addressed the meeting. Hitler made a special point of welcoming the Labor Service men from Austria, who were attending the rally for the first time.[13]

Konrad Henlein, the leader of the Sudeten Germans, had an interview with Hitler after the Labor Service parade and then abruptly left Nuremberg. He returned the following day. It was assumed that he had been sent home to warn his aides that their actions were embarrassing the Fuehrer, who was attempting to negotiate through the British.[14]

After the interview with Henlein, Hitler received the foreign diplomats for tea. At this gathering, André François-Poncet, the French Ambassador, gently chided him about Nazi truculence. The Ambassador observed that although the democracies were usually treated roughly in speeches at the Nuremberg party congresses, their representatives were welcomed. Hitler smiled and assured the Ambassador that they always would be, adding: "I trust that no mother will ever have cause to weep in consequence of any action of mine."[15]

The following day was declared the Day of Fellowship. Delegates from all factions of the party met in the Zeppelinwiese for athletic exercises designed to demonstrate the spirit of community among the movement's ranks.[16]

In the afternoon, the congress met to hear reports on recent developments in the German economy. The first speaker was Fritz Todt. He presented to the congress statistics on progress in road construction during the past year. He pointed out that thousands of miles of Autobahn had been created, and he outlined some of the important plans for the immediate future. Since the *Anschluss,* an Autobahn connection between Munich and Vienna via Salzburg and Linz had top priority. Among the other projects Todt mentioned were plans for a subway system in Munich, an enlargement of the Hamburg harbor, and 4,000 miles of road repair in Austria.[17]

Hans Frank, the Commissioner of Justice, predicted in his speech that the "criminals of the Dollfuss and Schuschnigg regime" would be proved guilty before the entire world in proceedings whose justness would be "incontestable." Frank spoke about the elevation of marriage (now under the aegis of the state, rather than of the church) and about the decline in the crime rate (as compared with the increase in crime in the "so-called democracies"—he was applauded when he quoted a U.S. Senate report to the effect that $13 million was paid annually to racketeers in the United States). Never before, he said, had people been as secure as they were under the Nazi regime.[18]

The day concluded with the annual torchlight parade of political leaders.[19]

Friday, September 9, was devoted to the political leaders. A number of committee meetings were held by the political leadership of various organizations. The two most significant gatherings were the sessions of the congress during the day and the large assembly of political leaders in the Zeppelinwiese at night.[20]

Walther Darré, the Minister of Agriculture, reported on the results of Germany's drive for agricultural self-sufficiency. He cited figures to back up Hitler's claim that Germany had stored enough food to last for years. He declared that the nation had a surplus of bread grain that could last two years. In addition, frozen meat and other meat conserves had risen from 5,000 tons in July, 1936, to 62,500 tons. During the same period, stored meat fats had doubled. The statistics he read on the supplies of vegetable fats, fodder, and potatoes were also impressive. Konstantin Hierl and Max Amann presented brief reports to the assembly. Mrs.

Scholtz-Klink announced that German girls would be encouraged to give two years of voluntary service to the state as nurse's aides, kindergarten workers, and social workers; they would not receive jobs in government and private industry unless they had served voluntarily for at least a year.[21]

The rally of the political leaders later in the evening was conducted with the same theatrics and pomp that had stunned the world in previous years. The total attendance this year had increased by 30,000. The hundreds of searchlights that created a dome-like effect over the field were, as usual, breathtaking. *The New York Times* quoted one American visitor as saying that the spectacle would make Hollywood bite its nails, because it was inimitable.[22]

The highlight of the evening was Hitler's address, which was noteworthy for one statement. Hitler expressed satisfaction at having before him 180,000 loyal, unswerving followers in this hour when war clouds were gathering on the horizon.[23] He was undoubtedly referring to the crisis in Czechoslovakia, but it was only one year later, almost to the day, that Hitler's armies overran the borders of Poland.

Hitler Youth Day was celebrated on September 10, as 38,000 youngsters gathered early in the morning for a rally in the Stadium. Baldur von Schirach opened the ceremony and introduced Hitler as the principal speaker. Hitler told his audience how different life had been for Germans of earlier generations, how little hope there had been for the future, how confined they had been within the limits of the class into which they had been born.[24] He assured them that all these bonds had been broken now, that youth was looked upon by the nation as its most precious guarantee for a great future. To be young in this new society, he told them, meant to look forward with hope to a promising and secure future. Rudolf Hess closed the meeting with a few words.[25]

The more militant spirit stirring in the party that fall had not been evident in Hitler's remarks at the youth rally, but it was expressed with bluntness and arrogance by Marshal Goering later that morning in a speech to the delegates of the Labor Front. Goering went beyond Hitler's careful, restrained warning to nations not in accord with German policy in Czechoslovakia and elsewhere. Speaking of the democracies, he said: if they do not like what we are doing, let them come out and fight; we are ready and cannot be beaten. Goering claimed full success for his Four-Year Plan after only two years. Germany, he said, had already stored up enough food and raw material reserves to last seven months without other supplies, so the threat of a blockade no longer frightened her. He admitted that hundreds of thousands of laborers had been commandeered for work, and that this had caused some discontent. A certain amount of forced labor was necessary because Germany had no colonies or native laborers. He hinted that the whole nation might have to work overtime for the glory of the Reich. The concentration of all Germany's energies on her most vital tasks was the demand of the hour. If he took men away from their homes and families, it was for their children's good.

The Czechoslovakian problem he characterized as one of a small section of Europe pestering its minorities and causing internal and international unrest. But Moscow and the eternal Jewish devils' grimace were behind it. He described the Czechs as "a little chit of a race devoid of culture." As for Czechoslovakia's friends, he advised Britain to establish peace in "that little Jewish state of hers" (he meant Palestine), although if she did, she would only have another war somewhere else in her regime—she always did.

The spirit of challenge that ran through the speech is summed up best in this passage: "We are well supplied and excellently armed. We have a powerful army and a great navy, and our air force is the world's most modern, most technically advanced, and most numerous. This air force justifies unshakable confidence in victory, and our fortifications in the West will halt any power under the sun. This nation of peasants and workers stands firm, threats have no effect on us." The conclusion of the speech was: trust Hitler, he has always been right and successful, and God has blessed him.[26]

The New York Times reported that this two-hour speech was received with great enthusiasm, and that the cheers lasted for several minutes after Goering sat down.[27]

During the congress session that afternoon, Secretary of State Fritz Reinhardt addressed the assembly with suggestions on how to overcome the decline in the birth rate by encouraging marriage and offering substantial government aid to ease family financial obligations.

Dr. Ley reported on the state of the economy, quoting endless statistics on prices, employment, social security, and so forth.

Goebbels added his voice, pouring scorn on democracy and its offspring, Bolshevism. He repeated his argument that freedom of the press was in reality nonexistent. He criticized former U.S. Ambassador William E. Dodd, who had decried the decay of German culture. Goebbels asserted that the Communist International had decided that Czechoslovakia should become another Communist stronghold in Central Europe. He charged that President Eduard Beneš owed his election to the Communist vote.[28]

The next day was the Day of the Storm Troopers. The program was filled with the usual rallies, marches, committee meetings, and speeches. Again there was a reminder of the unsolved crisis in Hitler's address to his political army. Two hours later, 150,000 Storm Troopers assembled in the Luitpold Arena. Hitler welcomed the Austrians into Greater Germany and then turned to the question of the Sudeten Germans, who were not as "fortunate." He said: "A new Germany stands before us, and we have the good fortune to live in it. To other Germans this still is denied for the time being. Our hearts go out to them, just as we know their hearts are with us and they are in spirit right among us."[29]

After the outdoor rally in the Luitpold Arena, the participants began to organize for their traditional march into downtown Nuremberg and the march past before Chancellor Hitler. Hitler stood in his car for hours with his arm raised.

Later in the afternoon, Hitler held a reception for the press. *The New York Times'* correspondent reported that Hitler did not discuss the political problems that absorbed him; he spoke only of his enthusiasm for art and architecture. On greeting his guests, he spoke first about the return of sunshine after the heavy rains of the last few days. "The rains," he said with a smile, "are good for the potatoes, but not for a party rally." He went on to speak of the beauty of Nuremberg. He said he was trying to clear its medieval section of all the trashy imitations that had been built in recent years and to restore its ancient charm. He pointed to the new projects the party was building for the annual rallies. He emphasized that this new city could be entirely separate from the old Nuremberg, with only a wide, modern avenue connecting them. "You will note, gentlemen," he remarked, "that we have made no attempt to continue the medieval style. The time for that is past, and such an attempt would produce mere trash." He went on to comment on the recent Munich exhibition of "degenerate art," which had aroused so much controversy when it was followed by a general purge of German museums. He said that Germany was quite willing to sell the objects exhibited to foreign countries if she got foreign currency for them. The money would not be used to purchase wheat or raw materials, but works by old masters; he especially wanted to acquire paintings by Dutch and Italian masters. He continued to chat about Nuremberg, comparing it to Florence, where he had stayed during his recent visit with Mussolini.[30]

Later in the afternoon, Foreign Minister von Ribbentrop gave a tea for Hitler's special guests. It was attended by representatives of the Italian Fascist Party, reporters from Japan, and other foreign journalists.

September 12 was the last day of the rally. As at former congresses, it was dedicated to the armed forces. In the morning, the troops were reviewed by their commanders; in the afternoon, they paraded before Hitler. On both occasions, at least 100,000 spectators, mostly men from various party factions, were assembled in the Zeppelinwiese grandstands. The army and air force were the chief participants, but there was a small navy contingent in this year's parade. The air force provided the novelties in the grand display. One was the first modern helicopter, which descended vertically in the middle of a sham battle, delivered a message, and took off again vertically. Another surprise was a group of four Fieseler-Storch planes, which landed in a small area directly in front of Hitler. They landed and took off at a speed of about thirty miles per hour. There were several new types of planes, including high-speed bombers and planes with twin fuselages. The program offered maneuvers similar to those of previous years.[31]

The military display served as an impressive background for Hitler's major speech at the congress closing session that night.[32] About 30,000 people heard the speech in the Congress Hall, and throughout the country millions of Germans listened over radio and loudspeakers.

Hitler demanded the end to the oppression of the Sudeten Germans. He said that they should be given the right to self-determination; he hinted that the Sudetenland would be claimed by Germany if its inhabitants wished. What had happened in Czechoslovakia could only happen in a democracy—the inhabitants were forced to accept the fabrications of the Versailles Treaty without being consulted. The world was told that the state had a special mission. The Czechs, Hitler said, had to find a pretext that would ensure their supremacy over other peoples in Czechoslovakia. Whoever opposed their supremacy was branded as a public enemy and, under the democratic system, considered an outlaw and beaten down or murdered. He stated that had Germans not been involved, Germany might have had little interest; but there were 3.5 million Germans in Czechoslovakia, a group equivalent in size to the population of Denmark. In an effort to rouse his audience's emotions, he described the conditions under which the Czechs forced these Germans to live. They were created by God, Hitler said, but not in order to be subjected to the hate and violence engendered by the Versailles Treaty; neither were 7 million Czechs created to discipline and torture Germans in the name of self-determination, as proclaimed by a certain Mr. Woodrow Wilson. The Sudeten Germans had been systematically ruined economically, he continued. The conditions under which they lived were fearful, the oppression terrible. The democracies ignored the injustice done to them, but it was not a matter of indifference to Germany. Hitler said that Germany had demonstrated her desire for peace by giving up large portions of her territory under the Versailles Treaty without ever planning revenge. But the oppression of the Sudeten Germans was a matter Germany could and would not tolerate silently. Since France and Britain had their own ways of upholding their interests throughout the world, Germany would claim the same right. Hitler denied the rumors that German troops were preparing to march on Czechoslovakia; he compared this with last year's claim that 20,000 German soldiers had landed in Morocco. These lies were a political strategy against Germany, and measures were being taken to ensure the security of the nation. Hitler said he had ordered an increase in the German army and air force; a line of fortifications along the Western frontiers was to be finished as quickly as possible. He referred to the West Wall, which he called the most modern defense system of all time, and he gave statistics on the grand effort being made toward its completion.

After Hitler had concluded his speech, the crowd responded with loud and wildly enthusiastic cheers:

At every pause the deep baying of the huge crowd gathered under the stars and the roar of "Sieg Heil! Sieg Heil!" supplied a sinister background. At last the one-time agitator of the Munich beer halls had the world for an audience. Yet, for all his tone of menace, Hitler was careful not to pin himself down; he demanded only justice for the Sudeten Germans and left in his own hands the decision as to what constituted justice.[33]

All observers agreed that the frenzy reached heights never before seen at a party rally. The excitement was carefully built up by Goebbels' ingenious propaganda machine. *The New York Times'* correspondent remarked that the enthusiastic participants returned to their home districts charged with new vigor and unlimited trust in their leader, for whom they were invaluable propaganda agents.[34] This was particularly important in the case of the ideas (they could hardly be called policies) that Hitler held on the Sudeten crisis. The masses at the rally had roared their approval of all his claims, all his threats. Hitler could rest assured that he would not encounter resistance to any action he chose to take against Czechoslovakia.

The international press reaction to this rally, and especially to Hitler's closing speech, was stronger than it had ever been. *The New York Times'* reporter wrote at the end of the meeting that it had been "more beautiful, if not more impressive than ever." He wrote a lengthy and thorough analysis of it for the issue of September 13, 1938. As before, the reporter was deeply impressed by what he had seen and heard, and he conveyed to his readers the feeling that he had just witnessed a political phenomenon of worldwide and historical significance.

Apart from *The New York Times,* the press all over the United States received Hitler's speech with the greatest interest. Many newspapers carried a complete translation of the speech; many printed extra editions. Across the country more than one hundred radio stations either carried the speech directly or broadcast translations of it. Wall Street was completely at a standstill shortly before closing time; the market prices could not be heard over the sound of the radio.

In other countries, the interest in Hitler's speech was also great. In Holland, Belgium, Denmark, and Finland, the speech was carried live, with simultaneous translations, and in all of these countries newspapers printed the full text. In Chile, Brazil, and Argentina, where the speech had been eagerly awaited, the papers brought out the text in extra editions.

When Hitler and his 950,000 followers left Nuremberg on September 13, they did not realize that they had attended their last rally. A huge arch had been erected at one of the major roads leading out of Nuremberg bearing the legend "Good-bye Until 1939." But on September 1, 1939, the German army invaded Poland, and the 1939 rally never took place.

15   THE PARTY DAY OF PEACE
1939

When participants returned home from the 1938 rally, the more
reasonable among them may have hoped, along with the rest of the
world, that Goering's threats and Hitler's hard, aggressive speech
were merely strong policy statements, and that international ten-
sions would somehow be eased. Prompted by Hitler's threatening
speech at Nuremberg, Chamberlain flew to Munich in order to
persuade Hitler to resolve the Sudeten crisis through negotiation
rather than force. During their meeting, Hitler seemed determined not to give in. He said that 300 Sudetens had already been
killed and he would under no circumstances let the situation continue. He demanded immediate settlement and stated that he
would think nothing of risking a world war. Chamberlain became
very disheartened and said that if Hitler had already made up his
mind to use violence, the meeting was a waste of time. Then, sud-

denly, Hitler seemed willing to discuss the secession of the Sudeten Germans from Czechoslovakia if the British would openly
back him. Chamberlain left to get the approval of his Cabinet and
to attempt to persuade Czechoslovakia to surrender the Sudetenland to Germany. Hitler, sure that Chamberlain would not suc-
ceed, quietly went ahead with his military preparations. When the
negotiations with Czechoslovakia became deadlocked, Chamberlain again visited Germany for talks with Hitler in Godesberg.
During this visit, the conferences with Hitler were clouded by fre-
quent reports of new killings of Sudeten Germans by Czechs and,
finally, news that Czechoslovakia was mobilizing.

On September 26, Hitler organized a mass meeting at the Berlin
Sportspalast, for the purpose of agitating public feeling against
Czechoslovakia. Three hours before the meeting, Chamberlain's
message reached him that the Czechs had refused to accept his
conditions. With this, his hysteria reached a high pitch, his speech a
masterpiece of invective which he would never surpass.[1] He committed himself before the nation and the world to stand by his
ultimatum: either Beneš would voluntarily give up the Sudeten
territory Hitler claimed or the German army would march into
Czechoslovakia on October 1 and smash all resistance. "Now let
Mr. Beneš make his choice!"

Despite repeated peace efforts by Britain and France, and despite strong warnings by his general staff against a war that could
hardly be limited to Czechoslovakia, Hitler sent his troops into
the Sudetenland on October 1. Under the pressure of Hitler's violent determination to risk a major war unless he could get the
Sudetenland, England and France gave in at the conference table
in Munich. It turned out later that Hitler had been bluffing, and
that his diplomatic tactics—which Churchill later called "demanding a pound sterling at pistol point"—had helped him achieve another major political victory in the eyes of Germany and the
world. Six months later, Hitler broke the Munich agreement and
overran the remainder of Czechoslovakia. Too late, the Allies realized that pacts and agreements with Hitler could not be relied
on; this rendered diplomatic relations with him impossible and
further increased the danger of war.

Soon after the Czechoslovakia crisis, a new conflict flared up,
this time between Germany and Poland. The cause of the mounting tension between them was the corridor linking Germany and
East Prussia and the city of Danzig which, under the Versailles

Treaty, had been given to Poland as its only access to the Baltic Sea. Again the German government played up rumors of mal-treatment suffered by Germans at the hands of the Polish authori-ties. When Hitler openly threatened to deal with Poland as he had with Czechoslovakia, Chamberlain, in an address to Parliament on March 31, 1939, gave Poland unconditional guarantees of support. Hitler, England, and England's allies spent the summer trying to line up as much diplomatic and military support as possible for their respective causes.

The Western Allies considered Russian backing essential in their conflict with Germany, and they left nothing undone in try-ing to secure it. Hitler, on the other hand, tried hard to get Italy to enter a military alliance, which he had planned for years. On May 22, the pact with Italy was signed, and it seemed that Hitler had moved another notch ahead in the diplomatic race with Eng-land. His success as a diplomatic manipulator was to grow even more spectacular. England failed to secure the much-needed agree-ment with Russia, but on August 23, 1939, Hitler, the great pub-lic enemy of Communism, signed, before the stunned eyes of the Western world, a nonaggression pact with Russia that kept his Eastern flank secure; it gave him unlimited freedom to deal with Poland without the danger of pressure from both the east and the west. This agreement later turned out to be a piece of matchless duplicity.

Through his high commanders, Hitler issued orders for prepa-ration against a possible clash with England and France over the Polish dispute; the preparations included defense of the German frontiers, organization of Operation White (war with Poland), and the seizure of Danzig.

Despite the pretentiously named "Pact of Steel" which Ger-many and Italy had signed, Mussolini was unwilling to declare war on Poland when Hitler decided to invade that country. He offered to mediate, but insisted that he could not afford to fight, since Italy was unprepared for war. Although Hitler must have been disappointed by Mussolini's refusal, he was wise enough not to let this break up the Axis. Despite last-minute efforts behind the scenes in Sweden, England, and Switzerland to save the peace, Hitler's army crossed the Polish border on September 1.

During the preceding summer, while Hitler and the Western democracies sparred for advantage, Nuremberg had prepared for a greater, more spectacular rally than ever. Despite Hitler's militancy in his conferences with the Allies, the organization committee for the rally went about its work, beginning early in July, as though oblivious to the danger of war. Ironically, the name for the 1939 rally was to have been the Party Day of Peace.

Everything about the 1939 rally was to have been grander than before. Thousands of laborers milled about the rally grounds all summer, building ten new tent cities for visitors. Others worked around the clock to finish the new concert hall, the big avenue linking the Luitpold Arena and the Märzfeld, and the great stadium.[2] The construction workers were fed in five large restaurants that had been set up near the party area.[3] A special force of 26,000 SS men was delegated to keep order along the marching route, direct traffic, and ensure that everything flowed smoothly.[4] For the first time, a new railroad station outside the rally grounds was to be used.

Other preparations for the 1939 rally were the following: a new route for the parade was made to control traffic; more than a thousand streetcar conductors were drafted from Vienna, Hamburg, Berlin, and Breslau; arrangements were made for the streetcars to go underground for a distance near the party area, a solution that was thought remarkably advanced; 150 kilometers of aquaduct were built for new lavatories; construction was begun on a special transformer to handle electrical current; 400 flags were made, each bearing the heraldic figure of a city of Greater Germany; in the center of the party area, grandstands had already gone up.

In late August, according to newspaper reports, the construction of the special camps was finished. At least 350,000 visitors were supposed to live in these camps, and 170,000 in mass quarters. The special train station was built, and the Reichspost opened twenty-eight special post offices. Approximately 7,000 singers and 2,000 musicians were to attend this congress. The timetables for 1,000 special trains were ready.[5] A detailed program had been worked out by the organization committee, and copies had been distributed to local party cells. According to *Fränkische Tageszeitung,* 2,500 participants had set out early in August on an "Adolf Hitler March" to attend the rally.[6]

On August 26, amid the hectic preparations for the congress, when thousands were already on their way to Nuremberg, the German news bureau in Berlin released the following curt announcement: "According to the press office of the NSDAP, the planned party rally from September 2 to 11 this year will not take place. Whether the meeting will be held later on depends on political circumstances." The government had planned to use a thousand special trains for the transportation of participants. Now, on the eve of conflict with Poland, all available trains had to be reserved for shipping troops and war material.

Only local party meetings were held during the war, since the war effort and, later, the threat of air attacks made national rallies in Nuremberg impossible. Party and Hitler Youth organizations continued to hold their regular weekly meetings, and on special occasions, provincial rallies were staged to celebrate such occasions as Hitler's birthday, the first day of May, harvest festivals, and the 1940 victory over France. The Hitler Youth held a mass meeting in 1943; there was also a loyalty demonstration for Hitler after the attempt on his life on July 20, 1944.

Yet even during the war Hitler dreamed of future rallies:

Nor will the rally lose its significance in the future. Indeed, I have given orders that the venue of the rally is to be enlarged to accommodate a minimum of 2,000,000 for the future—as compared to the million and a half of today. The German Stadium which has been constructed at Nurnberg and of which Horth has drawn two magnificent pictures, accommodates 400,000 people, and is on a scale which has no comparison anywhere on earth.[7]

And in conversation he remarked: "After the war, it will perhaps be best to have the columns marching past sixteen deep, and not twelve deep as hitherto. The march past would last four hours instead of five—and that would always be so much gain."[8]

After the war, the city of Nuremberg inherited the vast rally area—3 million square yards of concrete roads, fields, and finished and half-finished buildings. The area was an embarrassing memory for the city, and many plans were drafted for its use. The Luitpold Hall and the Luitpold Arena had been almost totally destroyed by bombs, and this area was converted into a park, with many flowerbeds. The Zeppelinwiese survived the war. American soldiers fenced in part of the field and used it as a baseball lot; they painted "Soldiers' Field" in white letters on the front of the grandstand. Later, a section was used for motorcycle and automobile races; this race track was called the "Norris Ring."[9]

The ambitious plans for the German Stadium were never executed. The construction did not get beyond a ditch sixty feet deep, which was kept free of underground water by a giant diesel pump that worked throughout the war years and was disconnected only when the Allies occupied the city. Within a short time, an artificial lake formed, which the people of Nuremberg dubbed "Silbersee."* The city rented the old Congress Hall as a storage building to several local firms. The unfinished new Congress Hall, however, presented a greater problem to the city fathers. The Nazi government had already spent more than 80 million marks on its construction. The walls were built of gigantic blocks of travertine; the cost of tearing down these monumental walls was prohibitive. Recent plans call for converting the structure into a semi-open-air auditorium seating 90,000 people. The giant avenue that connected the rally grounds and downtown Nuremberg was turned into a large parking area for visitors to the stadium. The huge towers of the Märzfeld were blown up at a cost of 2 million marks. Present plans call for an expansion of the Langwasser suburb into this area, which would create additional living space for 40,000 people.

The Nuremberg rallies will probably remain one of the most startling chapters of twentieth-century history. They are a frightening example of the awesome power of modern propaganda techniques. Borrowing from pagan cults, church rituals, and Wagnerian theater, and other ways of reaching the thoughts and dreams of the masses, the absolute state perfected, in Nuremberg, its ability to dominate man's mind.

---

* The name is taken from the title of a book known to every German schoolboy, *Der Schatz im Silbersee* (*The Treasure of Silver Lake*), by Karl May.

APPENDIX

Appendix
PROGRAM FOR THE PARTY DAY OF 1926

Saturday, July 3

4:00–6:00 P.M.   Meeting of the Special Committee of Reichstag, Landtag, and Community Delegates, in a hall of the Stadthaus restaurant. Chairman: Dinter. Speakers: Dinter, Frick, Fiehler, Amann.

6:00–8:00 P.M.   Meeting of the Special Committee on Problems Concerning Elections, at the Stadthaus restaurant. Chairman: Buttmann. Speakers: Buttmann, Streicher.

Meeting of the Special Committee on the Press, at the Stadthaus restaurant. Chairman: Ziegler. Speakers: Rosenberg, Ziegler, Amann.

7:00 P.M. Arrival of two special trains from Sachsen.

7:00–10:00 P.M. Meeting of the Special Committee on Propaganda and Organization, in the Ladies' Hall of the Armbrust restaurant. Chairman: Hitler. Speakers: Hitler, Goebbels, Suchenwirth, Heinemann, Strasser, Graber, Schulz.

9:00 P.M. Welcoming ceremonies at the main hall of the Stadthaus restaurant, the main hall of the Berggesellschaft, and the main hall of the Armbrust restaurant.

9:53 P.M. Arrival of the special train from Bavaria.

Arrival of the bands, and their parade through the city to the locations of the welcoming ceremonies.

Welcoming addresses in all three halls by deputies of the party leadership of Thuringia. Replies by Hitler, Strasser, Mutschmann, Goebbels, Rust.

Sunday, July 4

6:00 A.M. Reveille.

7:00 A.M. Ceremony of the SA and SS. Consecration of the flags. (For members of the SA and SS only.) German National Theater.

7:00–9:00 A.M. Meeting of the Special Committee on Civil Servants, in the lobby of the German National Theater. Chairman: Frick. Speakers: Frick, Schlange.

7:00–9:00 A.M. Meeting of the Special Committee on Finance, in the lobby of the German National Theater. Chairman: Schwarz. Speakers: Schwarz, Mutschmann.

7:30–11:00 A.M.	Meeting of the Special Committee on Women, in the Ladies' Hall of the Armbrust restaurant. Speaker: Zander.
7:30–10:00 A.M.	Meeting of the Special Committee on Education and Youth Organizations, in the Stage Room of the Armbrust. Chairman: Streicher. Speakers: Streicher, Rust, Bauer.
9:30–11:30 A.M.	Meeting of the Special Committee on Labor Unions, in the lobby of the German National Theater. Chairman: Wagner. Speakers: Wagner, Hildebrandt, Bachschmid, Stier.
9:30–11:30 A.M.	Congress of the delegates, in the German National Theater. Chairmen: Dinter, Feder, Strasser. Business report by Schwarz and Amann. Speech by Feder on fiscal matters and the economy. Thirty-minute intermission.
12:00 noon	Meeting of the congress resumes. Reports from the special committees. Speech by Goebbels on propaganda. Speech by Hitler on politics, ideas, and organization. Proclamation and closing address.
3:00–4:00 P.M.	Lunch for delegates at previously announced restaurants.
3:00 P.M.	The members of the SA and SS form two marching groups—Group A facing the Museum Platz and Sophienstrasse, Group B facing in the same direction at Paulinenstrasse.
4:00 P.M.	Parade begins. The route runs over the viaduct to the center of town.
5:00 P.M.	Mass demonstrations of all the participants in the Marktplatz. Speakers: Strasser, Streicher.

5:00 P.M.   Meeting of the delegates from Saxony in
                             the Erhölung restaurant.

6:00 P.M.   Meeting of the National Socialist Students'
                             Association, in the Stadthaus.

8:30 P.M.   Mass demonstrations: (1) At the main
                             hall of the Berggesellschaft. Speakers: Goeb-
                             bels, Strasser. (2) At the main hall of the
                             Stadthaus. Speakers: Buttmann, Streicher.
                             (3) At the main hall of the Erhölung.
                             Speaker: Dinter, on "The Christian Moral
                             Foundations of National Socialism." Dem-
                             onstrations to be followed by social gather-
                             ings in the gardens of the Armbrust and the
                             Berggesellschaft.

The timetable of the program must be followed exactly. Orders of
the police must be obeyed at all times. An information desk is located
in the hotel Preussischer Hof near the railroad station. Maps of the
city indicating all meeting halls can be purchased for 10 pfennigs at
the information desk.

Arriving groups and guests can make use of the guides assigned to
the railroad station in order to find their quarters in the city.

The leaders of party groups will receive written instructions on their
lodgings at the information desk. Those participants staying in mass
quarters are requested to bring their own blankets.

Guests using private quarters will receive instructions on their accommodations at the information desk. Rooms must be reserved in advance. The bill must be paid immediately upon arrival.

Smoking is prohibited in all mass quarters. Violation of this law
will be punished with a fine, and the quarters will be closed by the
police. Smoking is also prohibited in the National Theater by order of
the police. The party leadership asks that party members refrain from
smoking as a consideration to all speakers, and during the welcoming
ceremonies on Saturday, and at the demonstration on Sunday.

Each participant at the rally must wear the Party Day medal. The
medal should be purchased at the information desk immediately upon
arrival. Price: 50 pfennigs. This is the only contribution asked of
members toward the cost of the rally.

The congress of the delegates can be attended only by delegates
designated by local or provincial groups. Admission tickets must be
shown on request. Admission tickets for the delegates will be given

out immediately after arrival at the information desk. Proper identification is necessary. Price: 3 marks.

Lunch will be served in the gardens of the Berggesellschaft and the Armbrust from noon until 2:00 P.M. Price: 30 pfennigs for participants. Meals at 1.50–2.00 marks are available in the following restaurants: Fürst Bismarck, Stadthaus, Preussischer Hof, Erhölung, Chemnitius, Scharfe Ecke, and Klause.

PROGRAM FOR THE PARTY DAY OF 1927

Friday, August 19   Special committee meetings held in the afternoon.

Saturday, August 20   Opening of the congress.

                           Concert of brass bands at seventeen different locations.

                           Opening ceremonies in Nuremberg public squares. Torchlight parades in the evening.

Sunday, August 21   Consecration of the banners in the Luitpoldhain.

                           Parade of the SA and SS.

                           Closing ceremony of the congress. Policy speech by Hitler.

                           Mass meeting in the evening.

                           Concert of brass bands in the park of the Kulturvereinshaus.

PROGRAM FOR THE PARTY DAY OF 1934

Tuesday, September 4
(The Day of Welcome)

Reception for the international press in the Germanic Museum. Speaker: Hanfstaengl.

Press reception in the Kulturvereinshaus. Speaker: Dietrich.

Reception for Hitler at the Town Hall. Speakers: Liebel, Hitler.

Wednesday, September 5
(The Day of the Opening of the Congress)

Congress meeting in the Luitpold Hall. Speakers: Hess, Streicher. Reading of Hitler's proclamation.

Meeting on cultural problems in the Apollo Theater. Speakers: Rosenberg, Hitler.

Thursday, September 6
(The Day of the Labor Service)

Review of the Labor Service on the Zeppelinwiese. Speakers: Hierl, Hitler.

Congress meeting in the Luitpold Hall. Speakers: Ley, Goebbels, Wagner.

Friday, September 7 (The Day of the Political Organizations)	Review of the political organizations on the Zeppelinwiese. Speakers: Ley, Hitler.
	Congress meeting in the Luitpold Hall. Speaker: Darré.
	Meeting of the Association for Aid to War Victims (NSKOV), at the Kulturvereinshaus. Speaker: Oberlindober.
Saturday, September 8 (The Day of the Hitler Youth)	Review of the Hitler Youth in the Youth Stadium. Speakers: Schirach, Hitler.
	Meeting of the Women's Association, in the Luitpold Hall. Speaker: Hitler.
	Meeting of the Labor Service leaders in the Kulturvereinshaus. Speaker: Hierl.
Sunday, September 9 (The Day of the SA and SS)	Review of the SA and SS in the Luitpold Arena. Speakers: Hitler, Lutze.
Monday, September 10 (The Day of the Army)	Congress meeting in the Luitpold Hall. Speaker: Hitler.

PROGRAM FOR THE PARTY DAY OF 1935

Tuesday, September 10

3:30 P.M.   Reception for the press, at the Kulturver-
                     einshaus. Speaker: Dietrich.

5:30–6:00 P.M.   The bells of all churches in Nuremberg
                     ring in the Party Day.

6:00 P.M.   Reception for the party leadership and
                     high government officials, at the Town
                     Hall. Speakers: Liebel, Hitler.

7:30 P.M.   Gala performance of *Die Meistersinger von
                     Nürnberg,* at the Opera House.

Wednesday, September 11

11:00 A.M.   Opening ceremonies of the party congress.
                     Speakers: Hess, Lutze, Streicher, Wagner.

4:30 P.M.   Laying of the cornerstone for the new Congress Hall. Speakers: Liebel, Hitler.

8:00 P.M.   Cultural meeting, at the Opera House. Speakers: Hitler, Rosenberg.

Thursday, September 12

10:00 A.M.   Review of the Labor Service on the Zeppelinwiese. Speakers: Hierl, Hitler.

2:00 P.M.   Meeting of the treasurers of the Hitler Youth and the BDM (girls' division of the Hitler Youth), at the Town Hall.

5:30 P.M.   Continuation of the party congress. Speakers: Rosenberg, Wagner, Darré.

8:30 P.M.   Formation of the torchlight parade of political leaders.

Friday, September 13

8:00 A.M.   Meeting of the party delegates from abroad, at the Apollo Theater. Speakers: Hess, Bohle, Klemp.

                                 Meeting of the National Socialist Students' Association, at the Katharinenbau. Speaker: Rosenberg.

8:30 A.M.   Meeting of the Organization for Ideological Indoctrination, at the Opera House. Speakers: Rosenberg, Ley, Frauendorfer.

9:00 A.M.   Meeting of the Association of National Socialist Jurists, at the Kulturvereinshaus. Speakers: Streicher, Frank, Fischer.

10:30 A.M.   Continuation of the party congress. Speakers: Goebbels, Ley, Hilgenfeldt.

1:00 P.M.   Meeting of the National Socialist Press Club, at the Town Hall. Speakers: Suendermann, Dietrich, Dresler.

2:30 P.M.   Meeting of the Association for Aid to War Victims, at the Kulturvereinshaus. Speakers: Oberlindober, Liebel.

Meeting of the Committee on Finance and Administration, at the Town Hall. Speakers: Schwarz, Saupert.

5:00 P.M.   Review of the political leaders, at the Zeppelinwiese. Speakers: Ley, Hitler.

8:00 P.M.   Meeting of the National Socialist Women's Association, at the Congress Hall. Speakers: Hitler, Scholtz-Klink.

Saturday, September 14

10:00 A.M.   Review of the Hitler Youth, at the Stadium. Speaker: Hitler.

11:30 A.M.–2:00 P.M.   Meeting of the Labor Front. Speakers: Hitler, Ley, Schacht, Seldte, Schmeer.

12:00 noon   Meeting of the National Socialist Welfare Organization, at the Kulturvereinshaus. Speakers: Hilgenfeldt, Althaus, Mayerhofer, Laemme.

3:00 P.M.   Continuation of the party congress. Speakers: Amann, Todt, Frank.

Sunday, September 15

8:00 A.M.   Review of the SA, SS, and NSKK (National Socialist Motor Corps), at the Luitpold Arena, followed by memorial ceremony for the war dead. Speaker: Hitler.

11:30 A.M.   Parade, at Adolf Hitler Platz.

6:00 P.M.   Continuation of the congress. Speakers: Reinhardt, Dietrich, Hierl.

Session of the Reichstag, at the Kulturvereinshaus. Speakers: Goering, Hitler.

Monday, September 16

9:00 A.M.   Meeting of the political leaders at the Opera House. Speaker: Hess.

Meeting of the propaganda functionaries, at the Apollo Theater. Speaker: Goebbels.

Meeting of the Committee on Agrarian Policies, at the Katharinenbau. Speakers: Darré, Haidn.

Meeting of the Committee on Economic Policies, at the Kulturvereinshaus. Speakers: Koehler, Schaub.

Meeting of the Committee on Industry, at the Town Hall. Speakers: Todt, Staebel, Fruth, Seebauer.

Meeting of the Association of National Socialist Jurists, at the Town Hall. Speakers: Frank, Fischer.

First army maneuvers, at the Zeppelinwiese.

10:00 A.M.   Meeting of the Committee on Community Policies, at the Congress Hall. Speakers: Weidemann, Fiehler, Kerrl.

12:00 noon   Meeting of the National Socialist Teachers' Association, at the Apollo Theater. Speakers: Streicher, Kolb.

2:00 P.M.   Army maneuvers.

4:10 P.M.   Hitler addresses the army.

5:00 P.M.   Parade of the army, at the Zeppelinwiese.

6:30 P.M.   Continuation and conclusion of the congress. Speakers: Hitler, Hess.

9:30 P.M.   Taps, at the Zeppelinwiese.

PROGRAM FOR THE PARTY DAY OF 1936

Tuesday, September 8

3:30 P.M.	Hitler's arrival at Nuremberg.
	Reception for the press by Dr. Dietrich, at the Kulturvereinshaus.
4:00 P.M.	The old flags of the army and navy taken to the army camp.
5:30–6:00 P.M.	The Nuremberg church bells ring in the Party Day.
6:00 P.M.	Reception for Hitler in the Town Hall.
7:30 P.M.	Gala performance of *Die Meistersinger von Nürnberg*, at the Opera House.

Wednesday, September 9

9:30 A.M.	Hitler reviews the parade of the Hitler Youth from the balcony of the hotel Deutscher Hof.

| 11:00 A.M. | Opening ceremonies of the party congress, at the Luitpold Hall. Speakers: Hess, Lutze, Streicher, Wagner. |

4:00 P.M.   Opening of the exhibition "Political Germany." Sponsor: Hess.

Meeting of the NSBO and the Committee on Trade and Commerce, at the Town Hall.

Meeting of the Hitler Youth leaders, at the conference room of the Town Hall.

4:00–8:00 P.M.   Tent camp of the Labor Service is open to visitors.

8:00 P.M.   Cultural meeting, at the Opera House. Speakers: Hitler, Rosenberg.

Thursday, September 10

10:00 A.M.   Parade of the Labor Service reviewed by Hitler, at the Zeppelinwiese. Speakers: Hitler, Hierl.

6:00 P.M.   Continuation of the party congress. Speakers: Rosenberg, Goebbels.

8:30 P.M.   Torchlight parade of the political leaders through Nuremberg.

10:00 P.M.   Review of the torchlight parade by Hitler, at the Deutscher Hof.

Friday, September 11

7:30 A.M.   Meeting of the Association of National Socialist Jurists, at the Kulturvereinshaus.

8:00 A.M.   Meeting of the National Socialist Students' Association, at the Katharinenbau.

8:30 A.M.   Meeting of the Committee on Ideological Training at the Opera House.

9:00 A.M.   Ceremony for the National Socialist organizations from abroad, at the Hercules Hall. Speaker: Hess.

10:30 A.M.	Continuation of the party congress. Speakers: Reischle, Hilgenfeldt, Wagner.
1:00 P.M.	Meeting of the National Socialist press functionaries, at the Town Hall.
2:30 P.M.	Meeting of the Association for Aid to War Victims, at the Kulturvereinshaus.
	Meeting of the Committee on Finance and Administration, at the conference room of the Town Hall.
	Meeting of the party court judges, at the Opera House.
	Meeting of the Committee on National Health, at the Hercules Hall.
4:00 P.M.	Meeting of the National Socialist Women's Association, at the Congress Hall. Speakers: Hitler, Scholtz-Klink.
8:00 P.M.	Review of the political leaders, at the Zeppelinwiese. Speakers: Ley, Hitler.

Saturday, September 12

8:00 A.M.	Meeting of the Organization Committee, at the Katharinenbau.
10:00 A.M.	Review of the Hitler Youth, at the Stadium. Speakers: Schirach, Hitler.
11:30 A.M.	Meeting of the Labor Front, at the Congress Hall. Speakers: Hecker, Seldte, Ley, Hitler.
12:00 noon	Meeting of the Committee on National Welfare, at the Hercules Hall.
2:00 P.M.	Opening of the carnival, at the rally grounds.
3:00 P.M.	Continuation of the party congress. Speakers: Frank, Dietrich, Amann, Reinhardt.
8:00 P.M.	Fireworks.

Sunday, September 13

8:00 A.M.	Army maneuvers begin.
8:30 A.M.	Meeting of the Committee on Industry, at the conference room of the Town Hall.
9:00 A.M.	Meeting of the local propaganda functionaries, at the Hercules Hall.
	Meeting of the Committee on Agrarian Policies, at the Kulturvereinshaus.
	Meeting of the political leaders, at the Opera House.
10:00 A.M.	Meeting of the Committee on Community Policies.
10:30 A.M.	Meeting of the Committee on Industry, at the Town Hall.
2:00 P.M.	Army maneuvers continue. Speaker: Hitler.
5:00 P.M.	Review of the army by Hitler, at the Zeppelinwiese.
7:30 P.M.	Continuation and conclusion of the party congress. Speaker: Hitler.
12:00 midnight	Taps at the Deutscher Hof.

PROGRAM FOR THE PARTY DAY OF 1937

Monday, September 6
(The Day of Welcome)

Reception for Hitler at the Town Hall.

Reception for the press. Speaker: Dietrich.

Tuesday, September 7
(Day of the Opening of
the Congress)

Parade of the Hitler Youth.

Official opening of the congress. Speakers: Hess, Streicher. Wagner reads Hitler's proclamation.

Culture meeting. Speakers: Rosenberg, Hitler.

Wednesday, September 8
(Day of the Labor
Service)

Parade of the Labor Service. Speakers: Hierl, Hitler.

Continuation of the party congress. Speakers: Rosenberg, Hilgenfeldt, Wagner.

Thursday, September 9
(Day of the Opening of
the Athletic Games)

Laying of the cornerstone of the new German Stadium. Speaker: Lutze.

Continuation of the party congress. Speakers: Goebbels, Frank, Dietrich.

Torchlight parade of the political leaders, in the evening.

Friday, September 10

Consecration of the police flags. Speakers: Himmler, Hitler.

Parade of the police, in downtown Nuremberg.

Continuation of the party congress. Speakers: Darré, Amann, Todt.

Meeting of the Women's Association. Speakers: Hitler, Scholtz-Klink.

Consecration of the Hitler Youth flags.

Review of the political leaders, at night. Speakers: Ley, Hitler.

Saturday, September 11

Review of the Labor Front organizations.

Consecration of the NSFK flags.

Meeting of the Hitler Youth. Speakers: Schirach, Hitler.

Induction of qualified adolescents into the party by Hess.

Meeting of the Labor Front. Speakers: Ley, Goering, Hitler.

Conclusion of the athletic games.

Continuation of the party congress. Speakers: Ley, Reinhardt, Hierl.

Fireworks, at night.

Sunday, September 12

Mass meeting, and ceremony for the dead, at the Luitpold Arena. Speakers: Hitler, Lutze.

Parade in the afternoon, in downtown Nuremberg.

Monday, September 13 Review of the army, at the Zeppelinwiese. Speaker: Hitler.

Exhibition maneuvers of the army.

Rudolf Hess addresses the political leaders.

Closing of the congress. Hitler's farewell address.

PROGRAM FOR THE PARTY DAY OF 1938

Monday, September 5
(Day of Welcome)

Reception for the press.

Reception for Hitler, at the Town Hall.

Tuesday, September 6
(Day of the Opening
of the Congress)

Hitler reviews the flags of the Hitler Youth.

Opening of the party congress. Speakers: Hess, Streicher. Wagner reads Hitler's proclamation.

Presentation of the Imperial Crown Jewels to Hitler.

Opening of the exhibition *"Kampf in Osten"* ("The Struggle in the East"). Speaker: Rosenberg.

Culture meeting. Speakers: Rosenberg, Hitler. Award of the National Prizes for Art and Science.

Wednesday, September 7
(Day of the Labor
Service)

Review of the Labor Service, at the Zeppelinwiese. Speakers: Hierl and Hitler.

Parade of the Labor Service through downtown Nuremberg.

Continuation of the party congress. Speakers: Rosenberg, Hilgenfeldt, Wagner.

Thursday, September 8
(Day of Fellowship)

Athletic games.

Continuation of the party congress. Speakers: Todt, Dietrich.

Torchlight parade of the political leaders, in the evening.

Friday, September 9
(Day of the Political
Leaders)

Continuation of the party congress. Speakers: Hierl, Darré, Amann.

Meeting of the Women's Association. Speaker: Scholtz-Klink.

Review of the political leaders, at the Zeppelinwiese. Speakers: Ley, Hitler.

Saturday, September 10
(Day of the Hitler Youth)

Review of the Hitler Youth, at the Zeppelinwiese. Speakers: Hitler, Hess.

Committee meeting of the Labor Front. Speakers: Ley, Goering.

Final day of the athletic games.

Continuation of the party congress. Speakers: Ley, Reinhardt, Goebbels.

Sunday, September 11
(Day of the SA)

Mass meeting, at the Zeppelinwiese. Speakers: Hitler, Lutze.

Parade through downtown Nuremberg.

Monday, September 12
(Day of the Army)

Rudolf Hess addresses the political leaders.

Review of the army. Speaker: Hitler.

Exhibition maneuvers of the army.

Closing of the congress. Hitler's farewell address.

PROGRAM FOR THE PARTY DAY OF 1939

Saturday, September 2

3:00 P.M.   Hitler's arrival.

3:30 P.M.   Reception for the press.

5:30 P.M.   Church bells in the city ring in the Party
                       Day.

6:00 P.M.   Reception for Hitler, at the Town Hall.

8:00 P.M.   Opening of the "Strength through Joy"
                       festival by Dr. Ley.

Sunday, September 3

10:30 A.M.   The Hitler Youth reviewed by Hitler, from
                       the balcony of his hotel.

11:30 A.M.   Opening of the party congress.

12:00 noon	Open-air concert by military bands, at the market place of downtown Nuremberg.
8:00 P.M.	Gala performance of Wagner's *Die Meistersinger von Nürnberg*.

Monday, September 4

9:00 A.M.	Meeting of the Hitler Youth leaders, at the Town Hall.
11:00 A.M.	Continuation of the party congress.
4:00 P.M.	Opening of the exhibition "Wife and Mother—the Nation's Source of Life."
8:00 P.M.	Cultural congress, at the Opera House. Award of the National Prizes for Art and Science. Speakers: Hitler, Goebbels.

Tuesday, September 5

8:30 A.M.	Meeting of the Ministry of Education.
11:00 A.M.	Continuation of the party congress.
1:00 P.M.	Meeting of the National Socialist Students' Association.
4:00 P.M.	Meeting of the press functionaries.
8:00 P.M.	Open-air concert of SS music groups.

Wednesday, September 6

8:00 A.M.	Sports contest of the political leaders.
10:00 A.M.	Review of the Labor Service, at the Zeppelinwiese.
2:30 P.M.	Meeting of the Committee on Community Policies.
4:00 P.M.	Meeting of the Administration Committee.
4:00 P.M.	Meeting of the Association of National Socialist Jurists.
5:00 P.M.	Reception for the diplomatic corps, at the Deutscher Hof.
7:00 P.M.	Continuation of the party congress.

8:00 P.M.   Open-air concert by military bands.

Thursday, September 7

8:00 A.M.   Meeting of the Organization Committee.

8:30 A.M.   Meeting of the Association of University
                               Professors.

                               Meeting of the Special Committee on the
                               Ministry of Justice.

9:00 A.M.   Meeting of local propaganda functionaries.

11:00 A.M.   Continuation of the party congress.

2:30 P.M.   Meeting of the Association for Aid to War
                               Victims.

4:00 P.M.   Fellowship meeting.

                               Sports contest before Hitler, at the Zep-
                               pelinwiese.

8:00 P.M.   Torchlight parade of the political leaders.

9:00 P.M.   Hitler reviews the torchlight parade, at the
                               Marktplatz in downtown Nuremberg.

Friday, September 8

8:30 A.M.   Meeting of the Finance Committee.

                               Meeting of the Committee on Racial Poli-
                               cies.

11:00 A.M.   Continuation of the party congress.

4:00 P.M.   Meeting of the Women's Association.

5:00 P.M.   Closing of the sports contest, at the Sta-
                               dium.

8:00 P.M.   Review of the political leaders, at the Zep-
                               pelinwiese.

Saturday, September 9

8:00 A.M.   Meeting of the Committee on Agrarian
                               Policies.

8:30 A.M.   Meeting of the Ministry of Education.

9:30 A.M.   Review of the Hitler Youth, at the Stadium. Speaker: Hitler.

11:30 A.M.   Meeting of the Labor Front.

4:00 P.M.   Meeting of the Committee for Strength through Joy.

6:00 P.M.   Continuation of the party congress.

9:00 P.M.   Fireworks, at the Dutzendteich, on the rally grounds.

Sunday, September 10

8:00 A.M.   Hitler reviews a mass meeting of the SA, at the Luitpold Arena.

12:00 noon   Hitler reviews parade, in downtown Nuremberg.

Monday, September 11

8:00 A.M.   Exhibition maneuvers of the army, at the Zeppelinwiese.

8:30 A.M.   Meeting of the Committee on Industry, at the Town Hall.

9:00 A.M.   Meeting of the Welfare Organization, at the Congress Hall.

10:00 A.M.   Meeting of the local party functionaries, at the Opera House.

2:00 P.M.   Main event of the army exhibition, at the Zeppelinwiese.

7:00 P.M.   Closing session of the congress. Speakers: Hitler, Hess.

12:00 midnight   Taps by army bands before Hitler's hotel, in downtown Nuremberg.

NOTES

PREFACE

1. Alan Bullock, *Hitler: A Study in Tyranny* (New York, 1952).
2. Roger Manvell and Heinrich Fraenkel, *Dr. Goebbels: His Life and Death* (New York, 1960).
3. William L. Shirer, *The Rise and Fall of the Third Reich* (New York, 1960).

INTRODUCTION: THE CITY OF NUREMBERG

1. H. R. Trevor-Roper, *Hitler's Secret Conversations* (New York, 1953), p. 362.
2. Nadler has written a book on the recent history of Nuremberg called *Ich sah wie Nürnberg unterging* (*I Saw Nuremberg Destroyed*) (Nuremberg, 1959).
3. *Völkischer Beobachter* (Munich), September 1, 1923. All translations from German sources have been made by the author.
4. H. R. Trevor-Roper, *Hitler's Secret Conversations*, p. 460.

CHAPTER 1: THE FIRST PARTY DAY, 1923

1. Stephen H. Roberts, *The House that Hitler Built* (London, 1937), p. 135.
2. Alan Bullock, *Hitler: A Study in Tyranny*, p. 83.
3. See *ibid.*, pp. 60–61.
4. Information received from the staff of the Bavarian Radio, Munich.
5. *Völkischer Beobachter* (Munich), January 27, 1923.
6. *Ibid.*
7. *Ibid.*
8. *Ibid.*
9. *Ibid.*

10. *Ibid.*, January 31, 1923.
11. *Ibid.*
12. *Ibid.*
13. *Ibid.*

CHAPTER 2: GERMAN DAY, 1923

1. *Völkischer Beobachter*, September 1, 1923.
2. *Ibid.*
3. H. R. Trevor-Roper, *Hitler's Secret Conversations*, p. 145.

CHAPTER 3: THE WEIMAR RALLY, 1926

1. *Völkischer Beobachter*, July 3, 1926.
2. *Ibid.*
3. *Ibid.*

CHAPTER 4: THE DAY OF AWAKENING, 1927

1. *Völkischer Beobachter*, August 24, 1927.
2. *Ibid.*
3. *The House that Hitler Built*, pp. 135–36.

CHAPTER 5: THE PARTY DAY OF COMPOSURE, 1929

1. *Völkischer Beobachter*, August 6, 1929.
2. *Ibid.*
3. *Ibid.*
4. *Unheard Witness* (Philadelphia, 1957), p. 154.
5. *The House that Hitler Built*, p. 136.

CHAPTER 6: THE SETTING OF THE STAGE

1. These statistics are from the Bavarian Radio.
2. *Völkischer Beobachter*, September 2, 1933.
3. Information received from the Bavarian Radio.
4. *Völkischer Beobachter*, August 31, 1933.
5. *Fränkische Tageszeitung* (Nuremberg), September 8–9, 1934.
6. *Ibid.*, August 10, 1937.
7. *Guide to the Buildings of the Party Rally Grounds* (Nuremberg, 1937).
8. *Völkischer Beobachter*, August 1, 1933.
9. *Ibid.*, August 2, 1934.
10. *Ibid.*, August 30, 1935.
11. Information received from the Bavarian Radio.
12. *Völkischer Beobachter*, July 9, 1936.
13. *Ibid.*, July 16, 1936.
14. *Ibid.*, September 7, 1936.
15. *Fränkische Tageszeitung*, August 10, 1937.
16. Interview with Fritz Nadler, a Nuremberg journalist, in 1960.
17. *Fränkische Tageszeitung*, September 5, 1935.
18. John Baker White, *Dover—Nuremberg Return* (London, 1937), p. 39.
19. *Völkischer Beobachter*, July 15, 1936.
20. *Nordwestdeutsche Zeitung* (Bremen-Hamburg), June 8, 1937.
21. *Reichsparteitag, 1937* (Munich, 1937), p. 96.
22. Information received from the Bavarian Radio.
23. *Völkischer Beobachter*, July 16, 1936.
24. *Ibid.*, September 2, 1939.
25. *Ibid.*, August 14, 1939.
26. Information received from the Bavarian Radio.
27. *Fränkische Tageszeitung*, July 27, 1937.
28. Information received from the Bavarian Radio, 1960.
29. *Ibid.*
30. *Völkischer Beobachter*, August 14, 1939.

31. *Ibid.*, September 7, 1939.
32. Information received from the Bavarian Radio.
33. *Völkischer Beobachter*, September 1, 1938.
34. *The New York Times*, September 11, 1938.

CHAPTER 7: THE PARTY DAY OF VICTORY, 1933

1. Wilfred Bade, *Deutschland erwacht* (Altona-Bahrenfeld, 1933), p. 23.
2. *Völkischer Beobachter*, August 26, 1933.
3. *The New York Times*, September 1, 1933.
4. *Völkischer Beobachter*, August 26, 1933.
5. *Ibid.*, August 29, 1933.
6. *Ibid.*, September 1, 1933.
7. *The New York Times*, September 2, 1933.
8. *Ibid.*, September 3, 1933.
9. *Ibid.*
10. *Ibid.*
11. *Ibid.*
12. *Ibid.*
13. *Ibid.*
14. Eyewitness account of Miss Elisabeth Dettmann, who attended the rally as a Red Cross nurse.
15. *The New York Times*, September 4, 1933.
16. *Ibid.*
17. *Ibid.*
18. *Ibid.*, September 5, 1933.
19. *Ibid.*, September 6, 1933.

CHAPTER 8: THE PARTY DAY OF UNITY, 1934

1. *Völkischer Beobachter*, September 6, 1934.
2. *Ibid.*, September 5, 1934.
3. *The New York Times*, September 5, 1934.
4. *Ibid.*
5. *Völkischer Beobachter*, September 5, 1934.
6. *The New York Times*, September 4, 1934.
7. *Völkischer Beobachter*, August 5, 1934.
8. *The New York Times*, September 4, 1934.
9. *Ibid.*, September 5, 1934.
10. *Völkischer Beobachter*, September 5, 1934.
11. *Ibid.*
12. *The New York Times*, September 6, 1934.
13. *Ibid.*
14. *Ibid.*
15. *Ibid.*
16. *Ibid.*
17. *Ibid.*
18. *Ibid.*, September 7, 1934.
19. *Berlin Diary* (New York, 1942), p. 17.
20. *The New York Times*, September 8, 1934.
21. *Ibid.*
22. *Völkischer Beobachter*, September 8, 1934.
23. *Ibid.*
24. *Ibid.*
25. *Ibid.*
26. *The New York Times*, September 9, 1934.
27. *Ibid.*
28. *Ibid.*
29. *Ibid.*
30. *Reichstagung in Nürnberg, 1934* (Berlin, 1934), p. 354.

31. *The New York Times,* September 9, 1934.
32. *Völkischer Beobachter,* September 9, 1934.
33. *Ibid.,* September 10, 1934.
34. *The New York Times,* September 10, 1934.
35. *Ibid.*
36. *Völkischer Beobachter,* September 10, 1934.
37. *Reichstqgung in Nürnberg, 1934,* p. 364.
38. *Berlin Diary,* p. 18.
39. *The New York Times,* September 10, 1934.
40. *Völkischer Beobachter,* September 10, 1934.
41. William L. Shirer, *Berlin Diary,* p. 19.
42. *Völkischer Beobachter,* September 11, 1934.
43. *Ibid.,* September 8, 1934.

CHAPTER 9: THE CELLULOID IMAGE

1. These details on Nazi film controls are found in Roger Manvell and Heinrich Fraenkel, *Dr. Goebbels: His Life and Death,* p. 141.
2. *Hinter den Kulissen des Reichsparteitagfilms* (Munich, 1935), p. 84. Siegfried Kracauer writes that "this illuminating statement reveals that the convention was planned not only as a spectacular mass meeting, but also as spectacular film propaganda." *(From Caligari to Hitler: A Psychological Study of the German Film* [New York, 1946], p. 301.)
3. *The Saturday Evening Post,* March 30, 1946.
4. *Völkischer Beobachter,* September 2, 1933.
5. *Ibid.,* September 6, 1934.
6. The information on the following pages is from this book.
7. In a letter to the author, dated October 7, 1963. In the same letter, Miss Riefenstahl pointed out that because the generals felt neglected, she made a short film of the army maneuvers. This film, which was called *Day of Freedom,* was distributed by the UFA. According to Miss Riefenstahl, there are no copies available at the present time.
8. P. 95.
9. *Ibid.,* p. 300.
10. *Völkischer Beobachter,* March 31, 1935.

CHAPTER 10: THE PARTY DAY OF FREEDOM, 1935

1. *Völkischer Beobachter,* August 19, 1935.
2. *Ibid.,* September 3, 1935.
3. *Ibid.,* September 4, 1935.
4. *Ibid.,* September 5, 1935.
5. *Ibid.,* September 6, 1935.
6. *Ibid.*
7. *Ibid.,* September 7, 1935.
8. *Ibid.,* September 11, 1935.
9. *The Times* (London), September 11, 1935.
10. *Ibid.;* and *Völkischer Beobachter,* September 12, 1935.
11. *Völkischer Beobachter,* September 12, 1935.
12. *The New York Times,* September 12, 1935. The opening of the congress was also covered by the London *Times* (September 12, 1935), and briefly in the *Völkischer Beobachter* (September 12, 1935).
13. *The Times* (London), September 12, 1935.
14. *Ibid.,* and *Völkischer Beobachter,* September 13, 1935.
15. *The New York Times,* September 13, 1935.
16. *Völkischer Beobachter,* September 13, 1935.
17. *Reichstagung in Nürnberg, 1935* (Berlin, 1935), pp. 87 ff. References are also to be found in *The Times* (London) and the *Völkischer Beobachter,* both of September 13, 1935.

18. *Reichstagung in Nürnberg, 1935*, pp. 91 ff.; also *The New York Times*, September 13, 1935.
19. *Reichstagung in Nürnberg, 1935*, p. 162.
20. *Völkischer Beobachter*, September 14, 1935.
21. *The New York Times*, September 14, 1935.
22. *Reichstagung in Nürnberg, 1935*, pp. 234 ff.; and *The New York Times*, September 14, 1935.
23. *The New York Times*, September 15, 1935. See also *Reichstagung in Nürnberg, 1935*, pp. 244 ff.
24. *Völkischer Beobachter*, September 15, 1935.
25. *Reichstagung in Nürnberg, 1935*, p. 244.
26. *Ibid.*, p. 247; and *The New York Times*, September 15, 1935.
27. *The New York Times*, September 15, 1935.
28. *Reichstagung in Nürnberg, 1935*, pp. 247 ff.
29. *Ibid.*, pp. 270 ff.
30. *Ibid.*, pp. 290 ff.
31. *Ibid.*, pp. 296 ff.
32. *Ibid.*, pp. 305 ff.
33. *Ibid.*, pp. 360 ff.
34. *Ibid.*, pp. 372 ff.
35. *The New York Times*, September 17, 1935.
36. *Ibid.*
37. *Völkischer Beobachter*, September 14, 1935.
38. *Ibid.*, September 17, 1935.
39. *Ibid.*, September 16, 1935.
40. *Hitler: A Study in Tyranny*, p. 309.

CHAPTER 11: THE ORGANIZATION MANIA

1. A detailed article on the organization committee and the individual responsibilities of its members appeared in the *Fränkische Tageszeitung*, August 29, 1936, under the title *"Männer am Werk"* ("Men at Work").
2. Report by a participant in the 1933 rally, a member of a brass band.
3. Information given in an interview with Fritz Nadler, 1960.
4. Eyewitness report by a former member of a Hitler Youth choir.
5. *Kampfschrift der obersten SA Führung*, Vol. XII, Reichstag des Deutschen Volkes, pp. 123 ff.
6. *Völkischer Beobachter*, September 10, 1935.
7. *Ibid.*
8. Police regulations concerning the rallies. Nuremberg Archives, No. 4970.80.
9. Eyewitness report by a nurse who attended the rally.
10. *Völkischer Beobachter*, special ed., September, 1934.
11. Organization plan of the rallies, Nuremberg Archives, No. 4971.8.
12. This estimate, dated January 12, 1961, is in the author's possession.

CHAPTER 12: THE PARTY DAY OF HONOR AND FREEDOM, 1936

1. *Völkischer Beobachter*, September 5, 1936.
2. *Ibid.*, September 9, 1936.
3. *Ibid.*, September 5, 1936.
4. *Ibid.*, September 9, 1936.
5. *Ibid.*
6. *The New York Times*, September 9, 1936.
7. *Ibid.*
8. *Ibid.*
9. *Reichstagung in Nürnberg, 1936* (Berlin, 1936), pp. 54 ff.
10. *Ibid.*, pp. 62 ff.
11. *Völkischer Beobachter*, September 11, 1936.
12. For a detailed account of the events, see *Reichstagung in Nürnberg, 1936*, pp. 78 ff.

13. For a complete text of the ritual, see *ibid.*, pp. 77 ff.

14. For a discussion of the religious aspects of National Socialism, see Hans-Jochen Gamm, *Der Braune Kult* (Hamburg, 1962).

15. For a text of these speeches, see *Reichstagung in Nürnberg, 1936*, pp. 82 ff.

16. *The New York Times*, September 12, 1936.

17. *Ibid.*

18. *Ibid.*

19. A description of the meeting is given in *Reichstagung in Nürnberg, 1936*, p. 189.

20. *The New York Times* covered this meeting in great detail.

21. A detailed account of this meeting is found in *Reichstagung in Nürnberg, 1936*, p. 199.

22. *Reichstagung in Nürnberg, 1936*, pp. 210 ff. See also *Völkischer Beobachter*, September 12, 1936.

23. *The New York Times*, September 13, 1936.

24. See *Reichstagung in Nürnberg, 1936*, pp. 215 ff.

25. *Ibid.*, pp. 285 ff.

26. *The New York Times*, September 14, 1936.

27. *Völkischer Beobachter*, September 16, 1936.

28. *The New York Times*, September 14, 1936.

29. *Ibid.*, September 15, 1936.

30. *Ibid.*

31. *The House that Hitler Built*, p. 142.

32. *The New York Times*, September 15, 1936.

33. Eyewitness report by R. Michelowski, a Polish visitor to the rally.

34. *The New York Times*, September 15, 1936.

35. *The Times* (London), September 10, 1936.

36. *The New York Times*, September 15, 1936.

37. Alan Bullock, *Hitler: A Study in Tyranny*, p. 362.

CHAPTER 13: THE PARTY DAY OF LABOR, 1937

1. *Völkischer Beobachter*, September 5, 1937.

2. *The New York Times*, September 6, 1937.

3. *Ibid.*

4. *Völkischer Beobachter*, September 7, 1937.

5. *Reichstagung in Nürnberg, 1937* (Berlin, 1937), pp. 15 ff.

6. For the complete text, see *ibid.*, pp. 54 ff.

7. *Ibid.*, pp. 56 ff.

8. *Ibid.*, pp. 71 ff.

9. The most complete account is *ibid.*, pp. 89 ff.

10. *The New York Times*, September 10, 1937.

11. *Ibid.*

12. *Ibid.*, September 11, 1937.

13. *Ibid.*

14. *Ibid.*

15. The most comprehensive and vivid description of the meeting of the political leaders is given by Sir Nevile Henderson, in *Failure of a Mission* (New York, 1940), pp. 66 ff.

16. The texts of these speeches as well as a detailed account of the day are found in *Reichstagung in Nürnberg, 1937*, pp. 209 ff.

17. *The New York Times*, September 12, 1937.

18. *Ibid.*

19. *Ibid.*

20. A detailed description of these ceremonies is given in *Reichstagung in Nürnberg, 1937*, pp. 331 ff.

21. *The New York Times*, September 13, 1937.

22. *Völkischer Beobachter*, September 12, 1937.

23. This account is based on the report in *The New York Times*, September 14, 1937.
24. *Völkischer Beobachter*, September 13, 1937.
25. *The New York Times*, September 15, 1937.

CHAPTER 14: THE PARTY DAY OF GREATER GERMANY, 1938

1. *Hitler: A Study in Tyranny*, p. 399.
2. *Völkischer Beobachter*, September 5, 1938.
3. *Ibid.*, September 6, 1938.
4. *Ibid.*, August 31, 1938.
5. *Ibid.*
6. *Ibid.*
7. *Reichstagung in Nürnberg, 1938* (Berlin, 1938), p. 37; and *Völkischer Beobachter*, September 6, 1938.
8. *The New York Times*, September 6, 1938.
9. *Ibid.*, September 6, 1938.
10. For a full text of this statement, see *Reichstagung in Nürnberg, 1938*, pp. 63 ff.
11. *Völkischer Beobachter*, September 7, 1938.
12. *The New York Times*, September 7, 1938.
13. *Reichstagung in Nürnberg, 1938*, pp. 92 ff.
14. *The New York Times*, September 8 and 9, 1938.
15. *Ibid.*, September 8, 1937.
16. *Reichstagung in Nürnberg, 1938*, pp. 146 ff.
17. *Ibid.*, pp. 158 ff.
18. *The New York Times*, September 9, 1938.
19. *Ibid.*
20. *Ibid.*, September 10, 1938.
21. *Ibid.* For the texts of their addresses, see *Reichstagung in Nürnberg, 1938*, pp. 197 ff.
22. *The New York Times*, September 10, 1938.
23. *Reichstagung in Nürnberg, 1938*, pp. 238 ff.
24. *Ibid.*, pp. 238 ff.
25. *Ibid.*, pp. 247–52.
26. *The New York Times*, September 11, 1938.
27. *Ibid.*
28. *Reichstagung in Nürnberg, 1938*, pp. 292 ff.
29. *Ibid.*, pp. 340 ff.; and *Völkischer Beobachter*, September 11, 1938.
30. *The New York Times*, September 12, 1938.
31. *Ibid.*, September 13, 1938. For a description of the military maneuvers, see also *Reichstagung in Nürnberg, 1938*, pp. 366 ff.
32. For the complete text of this speech, see *Reichstagung in Nürnberg, 1938*, pp. 373 ff.
33. Alan Bullock, *Hitler: A Study in Tyranny*, p. 414.
34. *The New York Times*, September 13, 1938.

CHAPTER 15: THE PARTY DAY OF PEACE, 1939

1. Alan Bullock, *Hitler: A Study in Tyranny*, p. 422.
2. *Völkischer Beobachter*, August 13, 1939.
3. *Ibid.*, June 30, 1939.
4. *Ibid.*, August 15, 1939.
5. Information supplied by the Bavarian Radio.
6. *Fränkische Tageszeitung*, August 10, 1939.
7. H. R. Trevor-Roper, *Hitler's Secret Conversations*, p. 459.
8. *Ibid.*, p. 199.
9. A report by Heinz Böhmler of the Bavarian Radio.

BIBLIOGRAPHY

General Works

BAKER WHITE, JOHN. *Dover—Nuremberg Return.* London, 1937.

BULLOCK, ALAN. *Hitler: A Study in Tyranny.* New York, 1952.

DIETRICH, OTTO. *Hitler.* Chicago, 1955.

GOEBBELS, JOSEF. *The Goebbels Diaries.* Trans. and ed. by LOUIS P. LOCHNER. New York, 1948.

HANFSTAENGL, ERNST. *Unheard Witness.* Philadelphia, 1957.

HENDERSON, SIR NEVILE. *The Failure of a Mission.* New York, 1940.

HOFFMANN, HEINRICH. *Der Parteitag der Arbeit.* Berlin, 1937.

KRACAUER, SIEGFRIED. *From Caligari to Hitler: A Psychological Study of German Film.* New York, 1946.

MANVELL, ROGER, and HEINRICH FRAENKEL. *Dr. Goebbels: His Life and Death.* New York, 1960.

————. *Goering.* New York, 1962.

RIEFENSTAHL, LENI. *Hinter den Kulissen des Reichsparteitagfilms.* Munich, 1935.

ROBERTS, STEPHEN H. *The House that Hitler Built.* London, 1937.

SHIRER, WILLIAM L. *Berlin Diary.* New York, 1942.
———. *The Rise and Fall of the Third Reich.* New York, 1960.
TREVOR-ROPER, H. R. *Hitler's Secret Conversations.* New York, 1953.

Newspapers and Magazines

The New York Times (September issues, 1933–38)
Der Völkischer Beobachter (issues, 1923–39)
Illustrierter Beobachter (issues, 1926–29)
Fränkische Tageszeitung
Westfälische Landeszeitung
Nordwestdeutsche Zeitung
Fränkischer Kurier
Nordische Rundschau
Die Zeit
Niederdeutscher Beobachter
Deutsche Allgemeine Zeitung
Leipziger Neuste Nachrichten
Hamburger Tageblatt

National Socialist Publications

Deutschland erwacht. Altona-Bahrenfeld, 1933.
Reichstagung in Nürnberg. 6 vols. Berlin, 1933–38.

INDEX

ABOUT THE AUTHOR

Hamilton Twombly Burden was born in 1937 in New York City. During the war his family moved to Washington, D.C., where he was graduated from St. Albans School.

Mr. Burden has pursued his interest in contemporary history through independent study and research. The material for *The Nuremberg Party Rallies: 1923–39* was gathered over a period of several years. Mr. Burden traveled extensively in Germany, where he consulted many unpublished documents and interviewed local historians and eyewitnesses to the party rallies.

DATE DUE

5/10			
MAY 21 1968			
APR 1970			
APR 29 1970			
OCT 5 1970			
APR 27 1971			
APR 29 1971			
NOV 9 1972			
JAN 2 2 1973			
			PRINTED IN U.S.A.
GAYLORD			